Rethinking Vocationalism
whose work/life is it?

Rebecca Priegert Coulter
and
Ivor F. Goodson,
Editors

Canadian Cataloguing in Publication Data

Main entry under title:

Rethinking vocationalism

(Our schools/our selves monograph series ; no. 14)
Papers presented at the Transition from School to Work Conference held at the University of Western Ontario in Feb. 1992.
Includes bibliographical references.
ISBN   0-921908-15-6

1. Vocational education – Social aspects – Canada. 2. Vocational education – Social aspects – Congresses. I. Coulter, Rebecca. II. Goodson, Ivor. III. Transition from School to Work Conference (1992 : University of Western Ontario). IV. Our Schools/Our Selves Education Foundation. V. Series.

LC1047.C2R47 1993   370.11'3'0971   C94-930336-4

This book is published by Our Schools/Our Selves Education Foundation, 1698 Gerrard Street East, Toronto, Ontario, M4L 2B2.

For subscribers to *Our Schools/Our Selves: a magazine for Canadian education activists*, this is issue #32, the second issue of volume 5.

The subscription series Our Schools/Our Selves (ISSN 0840-7339) is published 6 times a year. Publication Mail Registration Number 8010. Mailed at Centre Ville, Montréal, Québec.

Design and typesetting: Tobin MacIntosh.

Cover design: Vidal Alcolea.

Cover photo: Typing class ca. 1933, courtesy of H. B. Beal Secondary School, London, Ontario.

Our Schools/Our Selves production: Loren Lind, Doug Little, Bob Luker, Tobin MacIntosh, Nick Marchese (Co-ordinating Editor), George Martell (Executive Editor), Satu Repo, Harry Smaller.

Printed in Canada by La maîtresse d'école inc., Montréal, Québec.
Copyright © Our School/Our Selves Education Foundation
December, 1993

Acknowledgements

This book and the February, 1992 workshop at which these papers were originally given were made possible through the financial support of The Social Sciences and Humanities Research Council of Canada (SSHRC), specifically a strategic research network grant in the area of "Education and Work in a Changing Society" awarded to scholars at York University, The University of Western Ontario and The University of British Columbia. The support of SSHRC is gratefully acknowledged.

We wish to thank *Studies in Political Economy* for allowing us to reprint the article "Subject to the New Global Economy: Power and Positioning in Ontario Labour Market Policy Formation" by Kari Dehli which appeared in volume 41, Summer, 1993, pp. 83–110.

We also wish to express our deep appreciation to Odilla Van Delinder for her technical and secretarial assistance in preparing the manuscript. And finally, we thank David Noble for reviewing the manuscript and providing useful editing suggestions.

Contents

Introduction   *1*
Rethinking Vocationalism

Chapter One   *10*
Reflections On The Role Of The School In The Transition To Work In Resource Towns
Jean Barman

Chapter Two   *28*
Structuring And Restructuring Vocational Knowledge: The Commercial Curriculum At The London Technical And Commercial High School, 1920–1940
Christopher J. Anstead and Ivor F. Goodson

Chapter Three   *52*
Constructing Vocationalism: Barbara, Darlene And Me
Jane Gaskell

Chapter Four   *69*
Schooling, Work And Life: Reflections Of The Young In The 1940s
Rebecca Priegert Coulter

Chapter Five — 87
Labour Education: Working Knowledge At The Core Of Learning
Jeffry Piker

Chapter Six — 95
Dropped Stitches: The Absence Of Domestic Labour In Discussions Of Schooling And Work
Madeleine R. Grumet

Chapter Seven — 113
Subject To The New Global Economy: Power And Positioning In Ontario Labour Market Policy Formation
Kari Dehli

Chapter Eight — 142
Restructuring Work: New Work And New Workers In Post-Industrial Production
Catherine Casey

Chapter Nine — 166
Rethinking Vocational Learning
Nancy S. Jackson

Chapter Ten — 181
Labour Unions, The Labour Movement, Working People: Resources For Ontario High School Teachers And Students
Jeffry Piker and Jim Turk

Dedication

For Kendra Coulter and Andrew Goodson
who now confront the new vocationalism
in their daily lives as students

Introduction

Rethinking Vocationalism
Rebecca Priegert Coulter and Ivor F. Goodson

Around the turn of the twentieth century, a new movement swept public schooling in both the United States and Canada. Now known conventionally as vocationalism, the movement was based on the belief that state-supported education ought to do more to prepare young people for employment and be more oriented towards the full range of occupational destinations. Reformers criticized the curriculum of elementary and secondary schools for being too academic and for preparing only a small minority of students for professions such as law, medicine, teaching and the ministry. Supporters of an expanded vocational education maintained that it was undemocratic to deny future industrial labourers, office workers, and homemakers the kind of schooling that would prepare them for the work they would do after they left school. Various forms of this debate about the role of the schools in preparing the young for work and life have continued throughout much of the twentieth century. Discussions flare up with particular intensity during times of economic hardship and high unemployment as is evidenced by current concerns with the nature and quality of schooling in Canada.

In recent years vocational education[1] in Canada has been much analyzed and assessed. Some historians, like T.R. Morrison, Timothy Dunn and Marvin Lazerson, have argued that vocational educators were more interested in training working-class pupils to be deferential, docile, and efficient industrial citizens than in equipping them with the manual and mental skills that would enhance their socioeconomic mobility or improve their lives.[2] Often contemporary critics of vocational schooling reach similar conclusions.[3] Vocational education is criticized for teaching students to be compliant and complacent workers and for training the young for low-skill, dead-end jobs. It is argued that the current emphasis on narrowly defined skills training in the vocational field maintains "the continuity of an approach that emphasizes the production, organization and regulation of human capacities to fit the existing social and technical relations and material conditions of the workplace."[4]

Nancy Jackson and Jane Gaskell, both authors in this collection, have contended also that while many of these same features characterize commercial and business education, a crucial variable was and is gender. Business education, by emphasizing the performance of standardized and routine office tasks and deference to the authority and needs of the (male) boss, has been implicated in the subordination and segregation of women in the paid work force as part of a larger and more general social process through which positions of power and privilege in twentieth-century capitalism have been reserved for some men.[5] Similarly, in his account of Adelaide Hoodless and the origins of domestic science, Terry Crowley has argued that the introduction of courses in dietetics, nutrition, sewing, and home management was essentially a "conservative" development which failed to challenge male dominance in the public world and reinforced gender roles that dated back to a preindustrial past.[6] As Dena Attar puts it, "For all its rhetoric, home economics has failed to empower the weak and the vulnerable and failed to advance women towards greater control of their lives."[7]

One common theme, then, in these accounts of vocational education is that industrial, commercial and domestic schooling was organized principally to discipline and control a large segment of the youth population earmarked for low-status and low-paying or no-pay jobs within a capitalist economic system. This theme of social control has been analyzed by Michael Apple over the past decade. For example, he argues:

> The formative theorists of the curriculum field [of vocational education], despite their identification with the middle class, increasingly viewed industrialization and the emergence of the corporation with favour. They were particularly enamoured of the seeming efficiency and productivity of industrial process and thus incorporated into their conception of curriculum construction the principles of scientific management that were thought to be responsible for it. But beyond this faith in corporate procedures, they were committed to its hierarchical mode or organization as *a model of society itself.*[8]

Perhaps the most explicit description of this vision of hierarchies was that of Finney:

> This conception of leadership and followship [sic] leads us again to the notion of a graduated hierarchy of intelligence and enlightenment.... At the apex of such a system must be the experts, who are pushing forward research in highly specialized sectors of the front. Behind them are such men and women as the colleges should produce, who are familiar with the findings of the experts and are able to relate part with part. By these relatively independent leaders of thought, progressive change and constant readjustment will be provided for. Back of these are the high school graduates, who are somewhat familiar with the vocabulary of those above them, have some feeling of acquaintance with the various fields, and a respect for expert knowledge. Finally, there are the duller masses, who mouth the catchwords of those in front of them, imagine that they understand, and follow by imitation.[9]

However, understanding vocationalism as a form of social control provides only a partial explanation of vocational schooling. It fails to do justice to the more complex historical and contemporary realities. Of course, vocational education has played a part in reproducing the inequities of class, race and gender in society, but vocational education can also be conceived of as a progressive force for change. In her chapter in this volume, Gaskell notes that women's groups and labour unions "saw vocationalism as an alternative to the existing elitist and male dominated curriculum, an alternative which might shake up the schools, include more working-class students, increase the respect given to women's work, and break down the barriers between mental and manual, theory and practice." For example, C.L. Gibbs, a master printer who became a teacher in Edmonton's Technical High School and a socialist Member of the Legislative Assembly in Alberta, argued in 1930 for technical education on the grounds that it would so imbue workers' children "with a sense of technical power and a confidence and a pride in their own creative skill that they will demand some share in construction and management compatible with their dignity as educated human beings."[10] Nancy Jackson's and Jeffry Piker's examination of labour education takes up the theme of respect for working knowledge and for the interests and concerns of working people. Piker argues that labour education reconstitutes the idea of "school" and reconstructs the relationship between school and work.

From the beginning vocational education was a category with contradictions. While the intentions of the dominant rhetoric and of the supporting constituency of dominant interest groups were and are clearly about occupational preparation narrowly understood, other forces were and are at work. That is, vocational education is an arena for struggle and for control over definitions, content and teaching methods. It is here that the book focuses on forces of resistance to the dominant interests and the subsequent development of patterns of reconstitution in vocational education.

Passing compulsory school attendance legislation, does not in itself ensure that young people of high school age will enrol in vocational education programs. Jean Barman's discussion of education in early Nanaimo and Wellington, B.C. demonstrates this point by outlining the resistance of young people and their families to schooling. So, if vocational education was to succeed among the nation's adolescents, it was necessary to generate popular consent for the basic message of vocationalism that schooling can most efficiently ensure the attainment of paid employment. As Barman shows, in a company town like Powell River in the 1920s, getting young people to stay in school was relatively easy since what the company wanted, the company got. That is, the company controlled the schools and the local economy and could enforce an explicit link between education and employment by, among other things, shaping the content of the school curriculum to fit young men for work in the pulp and paper mill.

The material benefits of vocational education were not so clearly identifiable in other communities. As a strategy to create popular support and consent in the early years of vocationalism, educators tried to attract the most successful academic students as well as those who ostensibly had the highest aptitudes for manual work. Proponents of vocational education publicized the capacity of the new curriculum to provide a general education consisting of an even balance between academic and practical subjects. By following this policy, it was hoped, large numbers of secondary school students could be convinced that a high school education at a vocational school would be a valuable academic experience as well as lead to gainful employment.

However, as we see in the study of the London Technical and Commercial High School, professional groups within the schools were engaged in a battle for status and resources which often caused them to stress academic content over vocational, thus reinforcing a particular kind of knowledge hierarchy. To ensure that a flow of status, money and resources came to them as educators, vocational teachers sought to include vocational education within the dominant rhetoric and existing structures of schooling. In doing this, teachers subverted the progressive potential of vocational education and, as Anstead and Goodson conclude, "the struggle for professional status resulted in a major increase in stratification and segregation in the technical school."

At the same time, individual teachers can reconstitute and reformulate their subjects in ways which fulfil the liberatory potential of good work education. By contrasting the content and teaching methods of *Barbara* and *Darlene*, Gaskell demonstrates how vocational education can either reinforce or challenge a dominant ideology and how students can be prepared to simply accept and fit into a workplace or learn how to change a workplace. Darlene's emphasis on understanding and on students standing up for themselves is a good example of the possibilities of vocational education. Historian Louis Schmier wrote of a similar approach in an informal homage to the typing teacher he had in 1956:

> Miss Trombly was not content with teaching us merely to learn how to type and take shorthand. As I look back, I think she was more interested in preparing us for life [than] for a life of typing and taking shorthand. There were no mindless Gregg typing or shorthand manuals to be found in the class. No chart of either the keyboard or the shorthand symbols — squigglies as Miss Trombly called them — hung on the walls.... Instead, the walls were so draped with printed quotations that they looked like pages from Bartlett's which she changed every week. There were no dull repetition drills. She expected us to learn how to set our fingers on the typewriter and learn the keyboard and learn the shorthand squiggle stuff on our own. In class, to sharpen our typing and shorthand skills — so she said — we copied bits and pieces she had selected from Hemingway, Greene, Faulkner, Rand and a few others! With about fifteen minutes left in the one hour class, she would stop us and ask what we felt about the passages we had typed. "Be a thinking person," she'd quietly admonish us if we hesitated, "not a living typewriter." ...To develop our shorthand speed and typing dictation speed, half the class formally debated issues while the other half struggled to record it. And we had to come in prepared to debate! As I remember, we discussed civil rights and racism, sex, communism, religion, democracy, etc.[11]

Students, whether individually or in groups, also may seek to resist and reconstitute the dominant rhetoric of schooling. This can be seen in a number of the papers in this collection. For instance, the work of Rebecca Coulter shows how young people persisted in their views that schools should prepare students for life and not just provide for narrow occupational training. In fact, during the 1940s and into the 1950s, students valued schooling but they did so for what they learned about politics, family life and the traditional basic subjects of English and mathematics, subjects which they identified as best preparing them for work.

Despite attempts by teachers, students and unionists to resist narrow understandings of vocationalism, it is plain that there are on going efforts to promote preparation for paid employment as the primary purpose of schooling. In this sense, linking school to work is an attempt to narrow the discourse around schooling. For instance, "school to life" or "school to lifelong education" or "school to social action" would present very different and broader discourses about the purposes of schooling, but we are not optimistic that such discourses will immediately prevail. Indeed, Madeleine Grumet's paper shows how whole areas of unpaid work and life experiences in the domestic realm have been and continue to be ignored by a discourse focused on school to paid work linkages.

In *Fluctuating Fortunes*, his impressive study of the political power of business in America, David Vogel has shown how the power of big business to inscribe public and political agendas fluctuates according to patterns within the economy.[12] As we review the situation currently, business is at a particularly powerful apex. Catherine Casey describes the growing capacity of global capital to define work and who will work and who will not. Her analysis suggests that conditions for the implementation of a corporate agenda for schooling and for vocational education may well be optimized.

Indeed, the patterns traced in the papers by Kari Dehli and Casey imply a period of rapid and potent change in workplace configurations which is likely to have a substantial dialectical effect on school to work relations. This is because much of the unremarked power of the school to work rhetoric is that it effectively argues backwards from "work to school." Hence when the workplace is being vigorously reconfigured, it is likely that the work to school/school to work relationship will also be rapidly and vigorously reconfigured. However, as Dehli points out in her study of Ontario labour market policy and the Ontario Training and Adjustment Board, we cannot predict specific responses and positions from any general analysis of global trends because "new domains of political struggle and different political subject positions are being constituted" as a result of the debates around work and training policies.

Dehli's position is closely linked to Jackson's call for a

"restructured vision of the 'vocational,' not only as a domain of educational action but as an important site of cultural transformation and political struggle." Jackson argues for a reconceptualization of vocationalism with an alternative theoretical framework that would challenge the discourse of productivity and global competitiveness rather than work within it. Like many others writing in this volume, Jackson is cautiously optimistic about the possibility of reclaiming the progressive and anti-elitist potential of vocationalism through the collective political work of the unions and other social movements.

As Casey points out, our relationship to work, whether through employment, unemployment or domestic labour, is central to our identity as human beings. It is precisely because of this that studying vocationalism is so important. How we understand the links between working knowledge, learning for work and working for learning will significantly affect our ability to make important political and strategic decisions about education in general and about vocational education in particular. The old questions about education — Who controls education? Whose interests are served by the education system? — assume new urgency in this era of global restructuring. By understanding vocationalism and through social action, it may be possible to change the answers.

NOTES:

1. In this introduction, the term "vocational education" will be used to include industrial education, technical education, commercial/business education and domestic science/home economics unless otherwise stated.

2. See T. R. Morrison, "Reform as Social Tracking: The Case of Industrial Education in Ontario 1870–1900," *The Journal of Educational Thought*, 8 (1974), pp. 76–110; M. Lazerson and T.A. Dunn, "Schools and the Work Crisis: Vocationalism in Canadian Education," in H.A. Stevenson and J.D. Wilson, eds., *Precepts, Policy, and Process: Perspectives on Contemporary Canadian Education*. London: Alexander, Blake and Associates, 1977, pp. 285–304; T.A. Dunn, "Teaching the Meaning of Work: Vocational Education in British Columbia 1900-1929," in D.C. Jones, N.M. Sheehan, and R.M. Stamp, eds., *Shaping the Schools of the Canadian West*. Calgary: Detselig, 1979, pp. 236–255; T. A. Dunn, "Vocationalism and its Promoters in British Columbia 1900–1929," *The Journal of Educational Thought*, 14

(1980), pp. 91–107. See also R.M. Stamp, "The Campaign for Technical Education in Ontario 1876–1914," The University of Western Ontario: Ph.D. dissertation, 1970. For the history of American vocationalism, see, for example, M. Lazerson and W. N. Grubb, eds., *Work, Youth, and Schooling: Historical Perspectives on Vocationalism: A Documentary History.* New York: Teachers College Press, 1974; H. Kantor and D.B. Tyack, eds., *Work, Youth, and Schooling: Historical Perspectives on Vocationalism in American Education.* Stanford: Stanford University Press, 1982; H.A. Kantor, *Learning to Earn: School, Work and Vocational Reform in California, 1880-1930.* Madison: University of Wisconsin Press, 1988; Jane Bernard Powers, *The "Girl Question" in Education: Vocational Education for Young Women in the Progressive Era.* Washington: Falmer Press, 1992.

3. See, for example, several of the chapters in J. Davis et al, *It's Our Knowledge: Labour, Public Education & Skills Training.* Toronto: Our Schools/Our Selves Education Foundation, 1989.

4. Roger I. Simon, Don Dippo and Arleen Schenke, *Learning to Work: A Critical Pedagogy of Work Education.* Toronto: OISE Press, 1991, p. 6.

5. Nancy S. Jackson and Jane S. Gaskell, "White Collar Vocationalism: The Rise of Commercial Education in Ontario and British Columbia 1870–1920," *Curriculum Inquiry,* 17 (1987), pp. 177–210; Jane Gaskell, *Gender Matters From School to Work.* Toronto: OISE Press, 1992.

6. Terry Crowley, "Madonnas Before Magdalenes: Adelaide Hoodless and The Making of the Canadian Gibson Girl," *Canadian Historical Review,* 68 (1986), pp. 520–547.

7. Dena Attar, *Wasting Girls' Time: The History and Politics of Home Economics.* London: Virago, 1990, p. 148.

8. Michael Apple, *Ideology and Curriculum.* London: Routledge and Kegan Paul, 1979, p. 77.

9. R.L. Finney, *A Sociological Philosophy of Education.* New York: Macmillan, 1928, p. 395.

10. C.L. Gibbs, "The Possibilities and Limitations of Technical Education," *The ATA Magazine,* XI (December, 1930), p. 5.

11. Louis Schmier, "Random Thoughts," Message on the Education Policy Analysis Forum E-Mail Network, May 23, 1993.

12. David Vogel, *Fluctuating Fortunes.* New York: Basic Books, Inc., 1989.

Chapter One

Reflections On The Role Of The School In The Transition To Work In Resource Towns[1]

Jean Barman
University of British Columbia

For some time I have been researching a company town that existed relatively unchanged for half a century, from 1910 to 1960, along the British Columbia (B.C.) coast. My particular interest in examining the history of Powell River has been with generational continuity. I want to know why sons did, or did not, follow their fathers into the pulp-and-paper mill that provided the almost sole basis of employment in the community. Increasingly, I have realized that I was simply assuming the role played by the school in the transition to the workplace, rather than stepping back to consider exactly what it might have been. The more I have reflected, the less certain I have become. What happened in the schools of Powell River and other resource communities may have done little or nothing to expand options in the workplace, and is this not, after all, what public education is meant to be all about?

The significance of such speculation goes beyond Powell River or even British Columbia. Single-industry or resource towns, many of them owned by private companies, have been a prominent feature of human settlement across Canada.[2] While their existence over the long term depends ultimately on national and international markets for the commodity being produced, quality of life within towns helps to determine not only economic stability in good times but the extent to which residents are willing to endure downturns in the interest of community survival. For families, one of these elements must be the character of the local schools, schools which ironically may have been limited rather than expanded options for their children.

To make the case, I want to relate two quite different vignettes of B.C. resource communities. The first comes from the coal mining towns of Nanaimo and Wellington in the late nineteenth century, the second from Powell River in the 1920s. Before doing this, I briefly want to review the history of public schooling as it developed in British Columbia.

The Development Of Public Schooling In British Columbia

A brief review of the development of public schooling in B.C. suggests that the system failed resource towns because, quite simply, it did not take communities like Nanaimo, Wellington and Powell River into account. Put another way, the "public" to which "public" education in B.C. was addressed did not extend as far as the "public" living in resource towns.

Public schooling in B.C. had its origins in the mid-nineteenth century. By the time B.C. joined Canada in 1871, consensus existed that the public education system should be modelled on Ontario, except that it should be non-denominational without special concessions for religious groups.[3] Control at the local level was vested in elected boards given various responsibilities including raising the proportion of school funding levied on property. B.C.'s provincial capital lay on Vancouver Island, and it was from Victoria that B.C.'s first intrepid Superintendent of Education John Jessop undertook his annual tours of inspection of each public school in operation across the far flung province. So far so good, but the system soon turned inward. Subsequent superintendents skipped the most distant schools, so much so that Barkerville with its origins in the Cariboo gold rush was not inspected once between the late 1870s and the turn of the century.[4] In line with the dominant rhetoric of the day, Jessop's successors were most concerned with efficiency and progress. The department's 1878 annual report asserted without equivocation that the principal measure of a school should be "whether it is efficient or not." School men equated efficiency with uniform curriculum, compulsory attendance, graded schools and the most modern buildings. These goals were most realizable in populous areas. Imposing new urban schools with their massive brick facades and glistening porcelain indoor plumbing so gladdened school men's hearts that they were described in annual reports in almost rhapsodic tones.[5]

Larger social and economic factors encouraged the move toward urban models. Not only Victoria but the province's other two largest cities of Nanaimo and New Westminster were located in the province's far southwestern tip. With the completion of the transcontinental railroad in 1886, its terminus of Vancouver came to dominance as B.C.'s principal metropolis and service centre. It too was located in the extreme southwest. By 1891 the area extending from Vancouver Island through Vancouver and the lower Fraser Valley contained almost 80 per cent of B.C.'s population, a percentage that has leveled off at about 70 per cent through the twentieth century.[6]

Thus, school men's urban assumptions only reflected the perspective of the majority of the province's population. What this majority wanted, so it was perceived, was more schooling which would then lead to greater employment opportunities. The first high school appeared in Victoria in 1876 and in the province's other three urban centres in the next decade and a half. Their initial programs of study were classical, intended as preparation for the professions or teaching. The Department of Education's goal was evident in the complaint of the principal of one of these feeder schools that he "was made to feel that my work was to pass pupils in to the High School and that my success in doing so would form the basis of the popular judgment as to my fitness for the position I held."[7] Reflecting school men's urban blinkers, only after the turn of the century did the first high school appear outside of the province's densely populated southwestern tip.[8]

In the early twentieth century some realization grew that the rest of B.C. had been ignored. School men's attention turned, at least perfunctorily, to what was perceived as the rural "problem." While the actual schooling that went on in the rural classroom did not move away from the dominant urban model, some shifts occurred. Superior schools were established, permitting children to continue through Grades 9 and 10, but high school education was considered more the exception than the rule. In the 1920s two surveys were carried out to ascertain teaching conditions in non-urban schools. By then or soon after, most prospective teachers were being given little lectures on what to expect when teaching in rural communities. The emphasis was on teachers coping with existing conditions as opposed to their using the school to effect change. Overall, what the Department of Education sought was to shift the blame for failure from itself to the locality, to rural trustees supposedly unconcerned to do anything, to uncaring parents and to irresponsible teachers. As J. Donald Wilson and Paul Stortz have elucidated, the initiatives were essentially gestures rather than a true change in direction away from urban priorities.[9]

This division of the public system into urban and rural obscured a third dimension. The special circumstances of children, more particularly boys, in resource communities were ignored. This cannot have been through lack of information. In the two 1920s surveys, for instance, teachers repeatedly referred to the uniqueness of company towns in particular. "Company town, School Board three company appointments." "Influence of company town very present." "This is one of the 'Company Towns.'"[10] Yet such key policy documents as the Putman-Weir Report of 1925, which set the agenda for public education in B.C. until after the Second World War, did not even mention resource towns. Company towns received passing attention and then only in the section on finance, where Powell River's "taxable real property" was deemed to be able to supply a greater proportion of school funding that currently the case.[11] Over 550 pages in length, the report focused almost exclusively on urban, mostly Vancouver, schools and to a much lesser extent on the perceived limitations of their small rural counterparts.

It may have been that from the perspective of school men, resource communities did not warrant attention away from urban priorities. From the late nineteenth century "the chief aim" of the schools was "to prepare the children of the Province, on entering upon the active duties of life, to become good and useful members of society."[12] The Putman-Weir report put the "general aim of education" as "to enable the child to take his place as an efficient participant in the duties and activities of life."[13] School men, rather than viewing their role as giving children the opportunity to choose how they should best become "good and useful members of society," may have confused means and ends. Students' ease in entering the work force in company and other resource communities may have been interpreted as a measure of success. In other words, the Department of Education was so determined to measure success in terms of outcomes that it lost touch with the means to that end. The consequence was that rather than expanding occupational opportunities for children, schools in resource towns narrowed them.

Nanaimo And Wellington In The Late Nineteenth Century

The first of the snapshots or vignettes to make the argument comes from the coal mining communities of Nanaimo and Wellington in the late nineteenth century. Nanaimo had its beginnings in the early 1850s when two dozen families were brought over from England to work nearby coal deposits. One of the first public schools to be established in the British colony of Vancouver Island was located in Nanaimo. As other mining communities grew up nearby, notably Wellington about five miles distant, so schools appeared there.

From the earliest days the schools at Nanaimo and Wellington refused to conform to school men's expectations, and they finally simply washed their hands of them rather than attempting to redefine their priorities to meet the special circumstances of resource towns. Superintendent Jessop noted despairingly in his very first report of July, 1872 that on the day he visited the Nanaimo school just 11 boys and 16 girls were present whereas the community likely contained about 175 children of school age. Numbers gradually rose but twice as fast for girls, and Jessop noted somewhat wryly that "there are probably as many boys as girls in the town."[14] In 1876 Jessop estimated that a fifth of the school age population was still not enrolled.

Those in school did not give cause for enthusiasm. "When the school was visited, the senior classes in both departments was little advanced in their studies. The boys were noisy and disorderly."[15] As would later happen with rural schools, Jessop put the blame squarely on parents. "A disposition on the part of many parents to send their children into 'the pit' at an early age is exercising a prejudicial influence on the rising generation by depriving them of the advantages of free school education."[16]

In 1876 the first written examination was held for admission into the new public high school just established in Victoria. Whereas 54 out of 70 Victoria students who took the exam passed, not one of the 26 sitting for it in Nanaimo did so. The average score was 277 in Victoria, 139 in the mainland city of New Westminster and just 53 in Nanaimo.[17] A year later no one from Nanaimo even bothered to take the high-school entrance examination. Jessop lamented:

> It is a difficult matter to raise and maintain a high standard of attainment in the senior division [of the elementary school] in consequence of pupils being withdrawn from school at a much earlier age than they ought to be. Parents should not under any consideration send their children into the mines, or give them employment above ground, till the before mentioned examination has been creditably passed.[18]

Over time, some Nanaimo boys did sit for the exam, but very rarely did the few who passed then go on to high school.[19]

In 1886 a high school opened in Nanaimo itself. Just 12 pupils enrolled. The problem lay, authorities acknowledged, in many being "engaged in pursuits by which they were enabled to support themselves or assist their parents."[20] In the late

1880s growing racism led to Chinese being prohibited from working underground. The school inspector lamented: "Owing to the exclusion of Chinese from the mines, a great many of our boys left school to fill their places, and consequently deprived us of some of our best material."[21] The high school by this time contained nine boys and 16 girls, whereas Nanaimo's elementary schools enrolled 430 children. Conditions changed little during the next decade, a typical condemnation from the visiting school inspector reading:

> The great inducements held out to boys of thirteen to fifteen years of age to work in the coal mines naturally draws a large number from the school every year, and place the senior divisions at a great disadvantage. You will notice, by the list of pupils, that quite a number of the boys of the age above mentioned have gone to work, thus carrying off the material that should go to the High School.[22]

Until the mid-1890s numbers in high school remained skewed by sex, 14 boys vs. 25 girls in 1892–93, 19 vs. 29 the next year.[23] Thereafter they levelled out.

If Nanaimo was bad, Wellington, just a few miles distant, was worse. Average daily attendance in the mid-1870s was just 25 per cent of enrolled children.[24] Labour unrest was greater in its mines than in those at Nanaimo, and insecurity of employment seemed to have equally negative consequences to Nanaimo's assurance of steady work. By 1877 Jessop had virtually despaired of parents:

> Family difficulties, arising out of the unfortunate colliery strike and disputes, have seriously retarded school progress in the district during the year. The result has been a very large amount of irregularity, a low average, and little or no advancement among the pupils.[25]

An atmosphere of hostility sometimes became open animosity against the school as an institution, as in 1885:

> For a long time the destruction of the school property has been a favourite amusement with the hoodlums of Wellington. The school has been repeatedly disturbed by them while in session; a large proportion of the windows have been broken; a number of panes have been entirely cut out; the locks were broken or

wrenched off the doors; the outhouses were destroyed; the stoves were broken into pieces and the stovepipe stolen &c &c In consequence of these proceedings, the school-house became in cold weather unfit for habitation. Every year the school-house, and its appurtenances, are renovated and restored; but immediately after these repairs the work of wanton destruction begins anew, and by the end of the fiscal year (indeed, long before that time) there is again little left but the bare walls.[26]

Unlike Nanaimo, Wellington boys could not be persuaded to sit the high-school entrance exam, much less contemplate attendance.[27] The school inspector commented that it was "not difficult to assign reasons for their comparative indolence." Again, the blame was fixed squarely on parents:

At an early age boys are able to earn in the mines (at employment requiring neither strength nor skill) almost as much wages as are given to adults in the Atlantic states. There is thus an inducement for parents to send their boys to work as soon as they are legally entitled to do so. On the other hand, if a boy distinguished himself by his proficiency at school there is no immediate prospect that he will be able to turn his acquirements to account. Suppose, as generally happens here, his parents are unable to support further expense in fitting him for a profession, then he must be a clerk of a teacher. In this Province clerkships, if at all valuable, are few and not so easily obtained. As to teaching, about as much money can be got by ordinary unskilled labour as is given in most of the schools to the majority of teachers. Under such circumstances is it to be expected that boys should be inclined to make painful and labourious efforts in the acquisition of knowledge?[28]

As the public school system as a whole turned its attention to efficiency and more specifically to the necessity for children not only to be enrolled but to attend school regularly, they found ever greater reason to despair of Nanaimo and Wellington parents. Expectations were set out in no uncertain terms by school men:

The allowing of children to be frequently absent from school on the merest semblance of an excuse, or on any avoidable pretext, tends to create in them a desire for freedom from the labours and restraints of the school-room, and too often causes the habit of irregular attendance to become chronic.[29]

Even tardiness could become a precursor of adverse lifelong habits:

> Want of promptitude in arriving at the school is a loss to the pupil of possibly one or more recitations of lessons, disturbs those who are punctual, is an annoyance to the teacher, and, what is worst of all, tends to cultivate the wretched habit of procrastination.[30]

Cases of "truancy" were always especially high in Nanaimo and Wellington. In 1880–81, for instance, 23 cases occurred among 310 enrolled boys in the provincial capital of Victoria, whereas Nanaimo recorded 70 cases among just 148 enrolled boys.[31]

The blame for conditions in Nanaimo and Wellington lay unequivocally, in the opinion of Jessop and his successors, at the local level. Not just teachers, but trustees were to blame.[32] Whereas trustees came in for repeated criticism for their supposed disinterest in school matters, the minutes of the Nanaimo and Wellington school boards paint quite a different picture — that of harassed boards trying to cope as best they could in the face of relative disinterest by provincial authorities. The Wellington board perennially operated on the financial margin. It repeatedly requested urgent help to keep the school open. "Our present school years grant is now presently exhausted and we stand at present indebted to R.D. & Sons for 6 1/2 tons of coal. The trustees do not feel justified in going any further in debt." We require immediate help from the Department "to unable us to continue school uninterrupted through out the term ... as the children cannot attend without endangering health."[33] Two years later Wellington trustees again sought rescue.[34] A year later they were in such dire straits that they could not afford to have the outhouses cleaned out. "There is an attendance of 300 children. The condition of closets can better be imagined than described."[35] The Superintendent of Education's response in this case seems to have been "to reduce staff to three teachers." According to the school board minutes, "trustees were of the opinion that present indications do not justify the reduction of staff to three teachers," but they could do nothing except to acquiesce.[36] Even while fighting off disaster, the Wellington trustees clearly believed firmly that their children should receive the best possible education. The board repeatedly expressed its concern over crowded elementary schools.[37] They came out against the use of corporal punishment for pupils "failing to have lessons" and wrote to the provincial ministry to see whether they could act in the matter.[38] The minutes do not record a response.

In nearby Nanaimo, the school board not only responded as best it could to local conditions, but repeatedly took initiatives to improve the level of schooling for all children. It contacted the Superintendent to see if kindergarten could be offered.[39] The answer was no.[40] The board requested that an unsuitable school text be replaced. The answer was no.[41] School attendance of 50, 60 and upwards to a hundred pupils in a single classroom prompted the board in November, 1891 "to write to the Supt. of Education drawing his attention to the overcrowded state of our schools, and the urgent necessity of having two assistant teachers appointed without delay."[42] The next spring one school was so full only standing room remained.[43] Shortly thereafter it was brought to the board's attention "that children have for some time since been refused admittance to the school and had to be kept at home for the want of school accommodation."[44] The board petitioned the Superintendent of Education and the city council for construction of additional facilities. The council refused to do anything, and the Superintendent sent only his regrets.[45] Eventually board pressure forced the council to change its mind.[46] Within half a dozen years overcrowding was again the issue. In one elementary classroom, "while there was only seats for 80 the actual average attendance for the past month had been 91."[47] The only solution, the board decided in 1899, lay in having "one half of these divisions attend school in the morning and one half in the afternoon."[48] Near the end of the year 60 elementary children were moved into the high school building, which was still underused.[49]

The impression left from juxtaposing the Department of Education's perspective with that of local boards is of a relatively intransigent provincial system so concerned with an urban model that it was unable to contemplate, much less respond to, any alternative set of circumstances. To the extent conditions eventually altered in Nanaimo and Wellington, it likely came through anti-child labour legislation which, it might be argued, was linked more to adult demands for employment that to pressure from the education system. The earliest regulations restricted boys under 14 from working underground except with special ministerial permission. After the turn of the century boys under 14 were completely banned from the pits. Even then they could still do clerical work above ground.

Powell River In The 1920s

The second, very different snapshot bearing on schooling in resource communities comes from the company town of Powell River. Powell River was an educational paradox. Externally its schools were eminently satisfactory, but this had little if anything to do with the province's role in schooling. An elementary teacher from the interwar years recalled in admiring tones that Powell River was the only school she ever taught in that had "two pianos." Such praise was exactly what the company that owned the town sought. Good schools were a very visible component of a deliberate policy intended to keep workers and their families acquiescent and quiescent. In the early 1920s trouble had erupted in the pulp-and-paper mill that dominated the town and the company was determined that it would not happen again. Workers had unionized at the time of the First World War. Between late 1921 and the spring of 1923 poor economic conditions were made the pretext to fire union leaders for supposed "disloyalty to the Company" and threaten to discharge the entire membership unless locals voluntarily disbanded.[50]

Once the unions were crushed the company set about putting in place the social infrastructure necessary to create what a Canadian company town planner of the 1920s termed "greater loyalty from ... more contented and efficient workers."[51] Company houses in Powell River contained the most modern conveniences at minimum rent. Even light bulbs were free. Workers shopped at the company store, ate eggs laid by company chickens and produce grown at the company ranch, swam at the company beach, read books from the company library, attended dances in the company hall, golfed on the company greens, played badminton in the company gymnasium, and gave birth and died in the company hospital. Powell River's children were central to the strategy. Workers had to be convinced that not only their future but that of the next generation was assured. Organizations like the Boy Scouts and Girl Guides were subsidized. The company's glossy monthly magazine, the *Digester*, which was distributed free to every household in Powell River, regularly included attractive photos of children of all ages from healthy babies to academically outstanding students and sports stars.

Powell River's schools were from the beginning under company control. The first school was opened as part of the company's initial construction of the mill in order to encourage families to move to the remote coastal site. By provincial law only property owners could sit on local school boards. Since the company was virtually the sole property owner, its appointed representatives were in effect the board.[52] The company's control over the system was assured by its payment of virtually the entire local assessment levied by the Department of Education.[53] School men basically removed themselves from any role in Powell River's schools, apart from inspection of what were by any measure eminently satisfactory facilities.

Indeed, Powell River's schools simply became better and better. As early as 1916 three pupils qualified for high school entrance. Three years later a superior school was established, making it possible to take the first two years of high school in Powell River.[54] By 1921 the superior school had proven so popular that it became a regular high school.[55] In June 1924 the entire completing class successfully wrote university matriculation exams, a distinction attained by just three other schools across the province.[56] The same autumn the *Digester* reported proudly the visiting high school inspector's pleasure "with the general tone of the school and the quality of the work."[57] The next year growing numbers of pupils led to the construction of a second elementary school, again located on company land and built with a generous injection of company funds.[58]

The company's goal was to retain as many of the second generation of males as possible in the town. Believing that the best workers were the best educated workers, the company's mouthpiece, the *Digester*, was straightforward in its admonitions to parents: "It is up to parents to keep the children at school as long as possible. It is an indisputable statement that the more instruction a child gets at school the better fitted the child will be for the battle for existence when maturity is reached."[59] To ensure that the "battle" would be fought in Powell River, curriculum were adapted to company purposes. In 1928 a two-month course in paper making was introduced into the high school curriculum as part of General Science. The Powell River mill made newsprint and the course's goal was for students to be able to place "the manufacture of newsprint in its proper perspective as only one branch of a very great and varied industry."[60] Two years later the course was expanded into a three-year technical program especially designed by company management in cooperation with the Department of Education's organizer of technical education to appeal to secondary students wanting to make a career in the mill.[61] Fully two dozen boys enrolled the first year.

Activities in the classroom were complemented by outside opportunities encouraging boys to identify with the town and its mill. Outstanding players on football and baseball teams, as well as in field sports, received letters, sweaters and shields from the school board, in effect from the company. Summer and weekend jobs in the mill were available to male teenagers in preparation for a permanent job once they completed their education. Preference was always given in hiring to local as opposed to outside applicants. Even where boys persisted in taking not the special technical course but the general academic course and then going on to university, they could count on summer jobs back home. At least some of them returned permanently in managerial positions.

In Powell River schools were an integral component of a resource company's larger agenda. While, as school board minutes testify, trustees regularly communicated their initiatives to provincial authorities, the local trustees were essentially the actors. The Department of Education's agenda, urban focused with a condescending nod to rural schools, probably made it grateful that Powell River demanded so little in terms of direct action on its part. Schools in Powell River did play a role in the transition from school to work, but only in terms of the agenda set by the company that owned the town. Alternatives were not encouraged, and the Department of Education did nothing to ensure that students were acquainted with occupational options. Rather, school men through their passivity assisted the company in its ongoing goal of maintaining control over the lives of workers and their male offspring.

Reflections

What then might we learn from these two vignettes? On the surface they appear quite different, not only in time period but in the quality of the schooling being provided local children. Their very diversity makes a fundamental point, and that is the social and psychological distance that has sometimes existed between public systems of education and the real world of resource towns. The measures that school men used to gauge schools' "efficiency" and "progress" were essentially those which could be quantified and standardized, from layout of buildings to records of attendance. They sought uniformity, a uniformity grounded in the urban models that appeared to them the most up-to-date and efficient, as well as the most visible from their base in the province's densely populated southwestern tip. Had they looked closer as opposed to wearing urban blinkers, realization might have come that the role of the school in some resource towns, as with Powell River, was not to open up opportunities in the workplace but only to fit the child to a particular workplace. This was certainly a situation in which many families concurred, but not necessarily one which the Department of Education ought to have indulged. Maybe nothing would have changed had school men included resource communities within their frames of reference. Maybe the appeal of the local workplace would have continued to take precedence. Because the public school system did not try and, as in Nanaimo and Wellington, did not even respond when localities sought assistance, we will never know.

An equally important question becomes what these snapshots tell us for today. Generalizing from the experiences of Nanaimo and Wellington and Powell River, it may be that to the extent education can expand horizons it will not occur through the school. The appeal of immediate employment may simply be too overwhelming. This perspective comes through in a recent survey of B.C. sawmills commissioned for the Council of Forest Industries and the International Woodworkers of America to measure employees' literacy levels.[62] Over two hundred employees, over 60 per cent of them born in Canada, were interviewed to investigate the extent of agreement between written workplace materials and employees' reading comprehension levels. The most interesting findings relate to the small proportion of workers having taken work-related training courses. Of the 70 per cent who had taken no courses, half said they felt "no need." Asked for the circumstances in which they would likely take a course, the two most frequent responses were "course needed to get better job" and "course needed to keep job." Practical, immediate utility holds the key.

It may be that, both in past and present, the central educational issue for workers in resource communities is not the transition from school to work but rather access to schooling at points of crisis. These will likely become more frequent, both as the Canadian economy redefines itself and as technology grows in importance. The number of jobs held by individuals with only a high school diploma or less is steadily shrinking as opposed to the growing number available to individuals with some post-secondary education. In the case of resource towns better access to post-secondary technical training and two-year colleges is clearly part of the answer, but so also is great sensitivity by public systems of education to the diversity of children's lived environments. As these vignettes from the late nineteenth century and early twentieth century testify, the particular circumstances of resource communities are not new. Perhaps we can learn at least a little from the experience of past generations.

NOTES:

1. The research for this essay was made possible by SSHRC (Social Sciences and Humanities Research Council) grants to the Canadian Childhood History Project and, more recently, a SSHRC grant to study generational continuity in Powell River. I am grateful to the SSHRC for its support and to my colleagues at the University of British Columbia (UBC) and members of the School-to-Work Network centred at York University for their comments on an earlier version of this essay. I owe a special debt to Helen Brown of UBC and Chris Anstead of the University of Western Ontario for their incisive critiques. A shorter version was presented at the Canadian History of Education Association Conference at Lethbridge in October, 1992 and I also thank those individuals who offered useful suggestions at that time.

2. The Canadian literature is summarized in Robert Robson, *Canadian Single Industry Communities: A Literature Review and Annotated Bibliography* (Sackville: Rural and Small Town Research and Studies Program, Department of Geography, Mount Allison University, 1986), and Rolf Knight, *Work Camps and Company Towns in Canada and the U.S.: an annotated bibliography* (Vancouver: New Star, 1975). Estimates of numbers of communities historically can be inferred from *Single-Enterprise Communities in Canada: A Report to Central Mortgage and Housing Corporation* (Kingston: Institute of Local Government, Queen's University, 1953).

3. See Jean Barman, "Transfer, Imposition or Consensus? The Emergence of Educational Structures in Nineteenth-Century British Columbia," in Nancy M. Sheehan, J. Donald Wilson and David C. Jones, eds., *Schools in the West: Essays in Canadian Educational History* (Calgary: Detselig, 1986), pp. 241–64.

4. Department of Education, *Annual Report*, 1876: 91, and 1901: 263.

5. See, for instance, Department of Education, *Annual Report*, 1894: 192 and 194–5 and 1895: 254.

6. For details, see Jean Barman, *The West beyond the West: A History of British Columbia* (Toronto: University of Toronto Press, 1991), Table 14, 371.

7. Department of Education, *Annual Report*, 1885: 316. Emphasis in original.

8. A high school opened in Nelson in January, 1901, followed by a second in Rossland in September, 1901 and a third in Vernon in January, 1902. Department of Education, *Annual Report*, 1901: 235.

9. Wilson, J. Donald and Paul J. Stortz, "'May the Lord Have Mercy on You': The Rural School Problem in British Columbia in the 1920s," *BC Studies* 79 (1988), 24–58, and Stortz and Wilson, "Education in Rural British Columbia: A Case Study of B.C.'s North-Central Interior in the 1920s," *Histoire sociale/Social History*, forthcoming 1993.

10. Department of Education, Teachers Bureau, School District Information Forms, 1928, Granby Bay, Westview and Woodfibre, held in British

Columbia Archives and Record Service.

11. J.H. Putman and G.M. Weir, *Survey of the School System* (Victoria: Province of British Columbia, 1925), 293, 297 and 299, also 20.

12. Department of Education, Annual Report, 1893: 626.

13. J.H. Putman and G.M. Weir, Survey of the School System, 44.

14. Department of Education, *Annual Report*, 1874: 17.

15. Department of Education, *Annual Report*, 1876: 94.

16. Department of Education, *Annual Report*, 1876: 94.

17. Department of Education, *Annual Report*, 1876: 128.

18. Department of Education, *Annual Report*, 1877: 19.

19. Department of Education, *Annual Report*, 1885: 313.

20. Department of Education, *Annual Report*, 1886: 144–45.

21. Department of Education, *Annual Report*, 1888: 199.

22. Department of Education, *Annual Report*, 1893: 542.

23. Department of Education, *Annual Report*, 1894: 199.

24. Department of Education, *Annual Report*, 1885: 324.

25. Department of Education, *Annual Report*, 1877: 19.

26. Department of Education, *Annual Report*, 1885: 324. The same thing happened in Nanaimo, although to a lesser extent. In 1893 the Nanaimo girls' school was broken into, doors damaged, some articles removed and a blackboard covered with obscene writing. Nanaimo School Board, Minutes, meeting of 6 November, 1893. Three years later windows were repeatedly broken. Nanaimo School Board, Minutes, meetings of 7 March and 12 December, 1896. In 1898 outhouses were damaged. Nanaimo School Board, Minutes, meeting of 22 October, 1898.

27. Department of Education, *Annual Report*, 1891: 183.

28. Department of Education, *Annual Report*, 1887: 222.

29. Department of Education, *Annual Report*, 1891: 261.

30. Department of Education, *Annual Report*, 1891: 261.

31. Department of Education, *Annual Report*, 1881: 270–71.

32. Department of Education, *Annual Report*, 1874: 17.

33. Wellington School Board, copy letter of 5 March, 1896, held in Nanaimo School Board offices.

34. Wellington School Board, copy letter of 19 March, 1898 to S.D. Pope, Superintendent of Education.

35. Wellington School Board, copy letter of 8 June, 1899 to Joseph Martin.

36. Wellington School Board, Minutes, meeting of 8 December, 1900.

37. Wellington School Board, Minutes, meeting of 9 December, 1896.

38. Wellington School Board, Minutes, meeting of 27 October, 1896.

39. Nanaimo School Board, Minutes, meeting of 5 October, 1895, held in Nanaimo School Board offices.

40. Nanaimo School Board, Minutes, meeting of 19 October, 1895.

41. Nanaimo School Board, Minutes, meeting of 3 and 10 April, 1897.

42. Nanaimo School Board, Minutes, meetings of 13 October, 1891 and 8 February, 1892.

43. Nanaimo School Board, Minutes, meeting of 8 April, 1892.

44. Nanaimo School Board, Minutes, meeting of 13 May, 1892.

45. Nanaimo School Board, Minutes, meetings of 12 March, 8 April and 8 July, 1892.

46. Nanaimo School Board, Minutes, meetings of 8 and 12 August, 1892.

47. Nanaimo School Board, Minutes, meeting of 2 October, 1897, also 1 and 6 October, 1898.

48. Nanaimo School Board, Minutes, meeting of 2 September, 1899, also 2 December, 1899.

49. Nanaimo School Board, Minutes, meeting of 28 December, 1899.

50. A. Lewthwaite, secretary of Local 76, Powell River, to John Burke, president of International Brotherhood of Pulp, Sulphite and Papermill Workers, 5 January, 1922, in correspondence between the local and international union, 1918–22. Copies held in the offices of Local 76, Powell River.

51. J.A. Walker, "Planning of Company Towns in Canada," *Canadian Engineer*, 53, 3 (1927), 147.

52. Initially one or two of the few independent property owners sat on the board, but by the 1920s it was entirely a company enterprise. For the history of schools see Alice Cluff, *Powell River and District Schools 1899-1983* (Powell River: Powell River Phoenix Printers, 1983).

53. Powell River School Board, Statement of Operating Expenses 1920–21, held by Powell River School District.

54. Powell River School Board, Minutes, annual meeting of 12 July, 1919.

55. Powell River School Board, Minutes, meeting of 7 September, 1921.

56. *Digester* 5, 1 (January, 1925), 8–9, held in Powell River Archives.

57. *Digester* 5, 1 (January, 1925), 8–9.

58. Powell River School Board, Minutes, meetings of 13 July and 7 December, 1925.

59. *Digester* 5, 9 (September, 1926), 9.

60. *Digester* 7, 9 (September, 1928), 19.

61. *Digester* 10, 1 (January, 1931), 2, and 10, 11 (November, 1931), 20.

62. COFI and IWA-Canada, *A Preliminary Study of Job-Related Communications Skills in British Columbia Sawmills* (Vancouver: JCP Research, 1991).

Chapter Two

Structuring And Restructuring Vocational Knowledge
The Commercial Curriculum At The London Technical And Commercial High School, 1920–1940[1]

Christopher J. Anstead and Ivor F. Goodson
University of Western Ontario

The first four decades of the twentieth century saw substantial transformations in systems of secondary education throughout North America. Social, economic and legislative changes brought new clienteles and new courses to schools in all regions of the continent. These adjustments inevitably altered the professional status (and thus the renumeration or working conditions) of teachers and educators associated with particular disciplines. In cases where status declined, one type of response employed curriculum change as a way to increase the material or symbolic resources available to subject teachers.

A case study of commercial studies in London, Ontario,

illustrates this intersection of curriculum change and subject status. During the middle of the 1920s two major changes transformed commercial studies at the London Technical and Commercial High School. This paper argues that these curriculum changes represented a response to declining subject status. During the quarter century preceding these changes, commercial studies in London declined from its position as a high status department in the prestigious Collegiate Institute, being first marginalized in that institution and then transferred to the technical school. These changes took place at a time when the subject's student clientele had become feminized and, with the transfer to the technical school, proletarianized. Commercial educators viewed the change in student characteristics as causing the decline in their subject's status (and thus in their own professional standing). They introduced two new courses in an attempt to change both the class and gender characteristics of commercial students. In the end, these initiatives led to an educational experience increasingly segregated and structured by class and gender characteristics.

The period of change in North American education from the 1890s to the 1930s has attracted a good deal of scholarly attention, furnishing a framework for understanding curriculum change in London, Ontario. In particular, the works of Herbert Kliebard, Harvey Kantor and David Labaree have provided clear elucidations of the patterns of conflict between various social and ideological forces involved in the construction of early twentieth-century American education.[2] Kantor and Labaree have both drawn attention to the semi-independent roles played by educators and students in the construction of curriculum; neither group acted simply as puppets of external interests. Both studies are particularly relevant to the present investigation: Kantor's because it examines the vocational movement, including commercial education; and Labaree's because it is firmly grounded within a case study of a particular school. In addition, Jane Gaskell and Nancy Jackson have produced a short study of commercial education in two Canadian provinces which provides crucial background to our exploration.[3]

The concept of subject status used in this paper emerges

from a definition used by researchers dealing with the status of individuals; this definition sees status as deriving from ownership of and control of access to material and symbolic capital. Subject status essentially represents the collective professional status of subject teachers. Its material side may consist of renumeration in cases where teachers in different departments receive different salaries. It can also cover career prospects, which may increase, for instance, when a subject earns departmental status. The material capital of a subject also consists of the collective resources in terms of buildings, classrooms and equipment which determine the working conditions for subject teachers. The symbolic side of subject status includes the authority or respect accorded to the subject, as well as the extent to which it controls access to a form of knowledge deemed valuable. This knowledge can be described in terms of cultural capital or credentials; its value reflects the degree of desirability of the opportunities for future prospects opened to the subject's students.[4] This paper further argues that, in the early twentieth century, a discipline's symbolic capital derived partly from the perceived value of the student body, and could change as a result of transformations in student socioeconomic characteristics.

Commercial studies, which moved from the Collegiate Institute to London's technical high school in 1920, underwent a major curriculum revision in the middle of the decade; as a result, the commercial course evolved from a single common general course, into three courses of different lengths, with different foci, aimed at different groups of students. The discipline had already experienced one major change at the start of the decade, when the provincial Department of Education ordered its extension from two to three years. According to principal Herbert Benson Beal, this allowed students to train for "the higher positions in mercantile life."[5] At the same time, the school allowed students the choice of leaving after two years with a "junior diploma" which Beal described as adequate preparation for "junior and stenographic positions."[6] At this point, though, all commercial students enrolled in the same general course. The first major exception to this rule took the form of a one-year "Special Commercial" course created in 1924. This course admitted only those students who already had several years of secondary school experience. It served to attract dozens of young women (and smaller numbers of young men) who had finished their academic education at one of London's prestigious academic schools — styled as "Collegiate Institutes" — or, in a few cases, other schools. Because these students had already obtained a grounding in academic subjects at their previous school, the special one-year course featured only strictly vocational classes.[7]

In 1926 the school announced the formation of a "Special Business Course for Boys," (which became a "General Business Course for Boys" in 1933). This new course had a different focus from the general commercial course; while the older course trained students to take general office positions, the new course trained male students for positions at wholesale firms and financial institutions, or in sales. As Beal pointed out, the course would prepare young men to work in places where they could find "ample opportunity for advancement."[8]

Why did these changes come about? One obvious hypothesis, that the provincial government insisted on their introduction, does not fit the evidence. Certainly, in both cases the provincial department allowed or authorized these changes, but they did not demand them. It was a purely local decision to take advantage of these options, and one which principal Beal seems primarily to have made. Neither the local Board of Education nor the Advisory Vocational Committee — which oversaw the school's operations — urged Beal in this direction; instead they simply reacted to his decisions. On the other hand, a lack of documents makes the question of whether Beal felt some pressure from commercial teachers in the school unanswerable, though that seems a reasonable contention.

Given that Beal (probably acting in conjunction with commercial teachers in his school) made the decisions to introduce these courses, what interests did they serve? If these educators established the new courses to serve the interests of the students, then they must have sought to change the school experience in some way. In fact, the two innovations did little to change existing practices. The special commercial course did not change anything for students at the technical school, since they could not take it. Instead of making improvements for an existing student clientele, the course sought to attract another group of students. Had this new group consisted of young people who would otherwise have left the educational system, the change would have represented a laudable attempt to build on the school's original mandate. The new course, however, did not seek out the otherwise unschooled, but instead aimed at attracting educated youths away from private business colleges or even from the Collegiates.

On the other hand, the creation of separate courses for males only marked the public confirmation of a pattern that had existed for years. From the first years of commercial courses at the technical school, the classes had a slightly different curriculum for each gender. The new course promised an emphasis on penmanship, business correspondence, accountancy, investment math and salesmanship; yet the commercial course already featured more of an emphasis on accountancy for males than females before 1926. The existing separate classes in other subject for each gender would have allowed for an emphasis on penmanship, business correspondence or investment mathematics if desired. The only real change in curriculum came with the introduction of a class in salesmanship; the introduction of a brand new course was primarily a feat of legerdemain.

The existing gender differences in curriculum fit into a wider pattern in the school (and of course wider patterns beyond the school); although all Ontario schools were premised on the American model of co-education, female students at the technical school followed a different curriculum from males.[9] Besides the obvious differences in the technical subjects taken by each gender, males at the school took algebra throughout their course, whether they had entered a general technical, matriculation or general commercial stream, while only those few females enrolled in the matriculation course took algebra, and they only took it from second year. In the technical department, females took art but males did not.[10]

Since the two new courses in no way responded to student demands, they seem to have been created mainly for the educators themselves. Commercial teachers did have definite occupational concerns at the time. In particular, they faced a clear decrease in the status of commercial studies, which occurred during the period from the turn of the century to the 1920s.

During the late nineteenth century commercial studies managed to amass substantial symbolic and material resources in the Ontario school system. From mid-century, classes in such business subjects as bookkeeping and penmanship became standard in the province's secondary schools. As demand for this sort of professional training grew during the second half of the nineteenth century, private business colleges proliferated, emphasizing a purely practical curriculum and guaranteed placement for graduates. The Ministry of Education also responded to this demand, introducing a one-year commercial course in 1885, and extending it to two years in 1896.[11]

In London at this time, commercial subjects made up part of the general academic curriculum at the city's Collegiate Institute. Commercial studies commanded increasing authority, and in 1895 became a separate department, with a distinct course of study, at the Collegiate Institute. In 1899 the commercial department moved to a new four-room building adjacent to the older C.I. building. From that point on, reports of attendance at the school listed students in the commercial department separately.[12] Both of these actions point to an acknowledgement of the amount of symbolic capital controlled by commercial education at the end of the nineteenth century; departmental status provided material resources in terms of additional teaching positions up to and including department head, while the new building represented a high standard of working conditions. Indeed, the incoming Chair of London's Board of Education confirmed this status in 1899 when he declared the primary role of the local system to be the provision of "a good English and Business education."[13]

The success of commercial studies in the late nineteenth century reflected the association of office work with middle class male respectability. Middle-class men in the late nineteenth century viewed clerical work as the first, obligatory, rung on a ladder of commercial success. Young men who wanted to make up the next generation of merchants, bankers or entrepreneurs, knew they had to serve their time as clerks, bookkeepers or secretaries. Many educators, worried about the movement of young women into the high schools, saw commercial courses as a way to make school more relevant and attractive to these male students.[14]

Though the achievement of departmental standing, and quarters in a new building, resulted from commercial studies' high status at L.C.I., the physical and administrative separation from academic subjects made the department much more vulnerable to marginalization as its cultural authority decreased during the opening decades of the twentieth century. At this time the symbolic capital associated with the value of the subject dropped throughout North America; thus the 1900 annual report of Ontario's Minister of Education quoted the opinion of the president of Harvard University on commercial courses, which he saw as "hopelessly inferior to other courses...."[15]

The physical resources which contributed to the status of commercial studies reflected the subject's large enrolment at the turn of the century; a province-wide decline in enrolment in the early twentieth century accelerated the decrease in subject status. In 1902, 11,334 students in Ontario secondary schools took bookkeeping among their subjects. By 1922, that number had fallen to 6,524. The increase in absolute enrollment made the relative decline in the attraction of commercial studies even greater. Almost half (46%) of Ontario's secondary students took bookkeeping in 1902; twenty years later, the proportion had fallen to less than 15 per cent.[16]

In London, the decline in commercial education's status led to marginalization, a process which started within the first few years of the new century with the establishment of domestic science classes in the commercial building, thus reducing the material resources controlled by commercial teachers. Domestic science classes were held in the commercial building from 1903, and by 1907 the commercial building had become too crowded. In 1908 the "severe overcrowding" had reached the point where one commercial class consisted of 62 pupils sharing 11 typewriters. Some of the pressure eased later that year with the transfer of domestic science classes to the basement of the main building. The commercial building remained crowded as it aged, and teaching conditions worsened. In 1915 the principal reported an average class size of 49, despite provincial regulations limiting class size to 30. By that point, the principal was talking of "separating the Commercial Department from the rest of the Collegiate work."[17]

After the end of the war, overcrowding at the commercial building reached a crisis point. In 1918 the Board authorized the removal of a staircase so classes could be held in a hallway, and the creation of a new classroom in the attic. Finally, in 1919 the Board decided to act. At first they considered a new building in a site distant from the C.I. since in their opinion, "it would be preferable to have the Commercial Classes entirely separated from the Collegiate Institute." When City Council refused to allow the funds for this, the Board decided to move the commercial classes into an old, decrepit, elementary school building, used by the military during the war; academic classes would move into the former commercial building. Even these poor quarters did not provide immunity for the commercial department; in September of 1919 academic classes which could not fit in the other two buildings took over one of the department's six classrooms.[18]

The transfer of the commercial department to the London Technical High School in the early 1920s represented another stage in the subject's downward trajectory. The technical high school had a remarkably different status from the Collegiate Institute, a difference based in the symbolic, rather than the material, realm. One of the chief factors behind the formation of the "London Industrial School" (later the "London Technical and Commercial High School") in 1912 was a desire to ease overcrowding at the Collegiate Institute by the transfer of students who only attended the school for a year or two, before entering the industrial workforce. Enthused by the claims of the movement for social efficiency, London educators undertook the implementation of a school which would prepare these students for their expected careers.[19]

Thus, from the start, the technical school suffered under the image of an institution for less desirable students. The school's first principal and prime mover in its creation, Beal, did not take this complacently. Instead he fought to raise the public's estimation of his school by attracting students who had achieved high school entrance standing. Beal wanted to challenge, and, in the end, destroy a widespread perception of technical schools as "the natural dumping ground for all backward and defective children."[20]

The willingness of both federal and provincial levels of government to fund technical schooling handsomely at this time provided an important boost to Beal's campaign, and brought control over considerable material resources to the school. The construction of a brand new building (completed in 1918) filled with up-to-date equipment, seemed to signal Beal's complete victory, and caused many traditionalists, led by the *London Free Press*, to attack the technical school on a variety of issues, all underpinned by a feeling that this new form of schooling presented a serious challenge to the cultural dominance of traditional elite academic education.[21]

The last of the campaigns of opposition took place in 1923 and early 1924. This campaign started with a series of attacks by the newspaper and council members which maligned the school in terms of its standards of teaching. Opponents also described the school as an inefficient part of the local system, claiming that it was too expensive and too little used. The climax of this campaign came with a movement to convert the technical school into a comprehensive high school, combining academic and technical streams. While this would have prevented the resulting school from challenging the Collegiate Institute on status grunds, it also promised to eliminate another problem — the growing need for some kind of secondary school in the city's predominantly working-class east end. The combined weight of technical education supporters, spokespeople for the east end community who wanted their own C.I., and provincial officials opposed to the comprehensive plan, finally scuttled this movement.[22]

Despite victories like this, and the early burst of funding from provincial and federal sources, any increase in status experienced by the technical high school proved short-lived. Neither of these factors led to any great increase in symbolic capital, since the key distinction between practical and academic forms of knowledge remained firmly in place. In 1926 the Board eliminated all the manual training and domestic science classes from the city's collegiate institutes (by that point the city had three C.I.s), making the distinction between these schools and the technical school more sharp.[23]

Beal's efforts notwithstanding, his school remained starved of symbolic capital. A teacher who arrived at the school in 1930 remembered how a "general feeling" existed "that you were rather an inferior type if you attended Beal Tech. It was for the people who just didn't have the ability or didn't belong to the right class of people." Or, put another way, "... if you weren't very bright you went to Tech. And [you also went] ... if your family was poor."[24]

Within a decade of the founding of this technical institution with continuing status problems, it became the new home of the commercial studies department formerly associated with the Collegiate Institute. The destruction by fire in April, 1920 of the C.I. building only hastened the implementation of existing plans to move the commercial students to the technical school. Within days of the disaster, administrators worked out a new arrangement; academic classes from the burned-out building moved into the classrooms occupied by commercial courses, and commercial courses moved to the technical school building. Though the commercial department remained administratively connected to the Collegiate for several months, the move proved permanent; the commercial department became an official part of the technical school a year after the fire and emergency move.[25] Commercial education, once a highly respected component of the L.C.I. curriculum, had now been consigned (along with domestic science and industrial education) to the technical school building.[26]

In 1924, facing this situation of declining status, commercial educators embarked on a set of curricular changes to increase the material and symbolic resources of their department. They had the full support of principal Beal, constantly concerned with his school's status, which had been seriously threatened in the previous 18 months. One way to increase the material resources of the discipline was to increase enrollment, resulting in a greater number of paid positions available to teachers of the subject and a greater voice in the distribution of other material resources. The provincially ordered expansion to a three-year course in 1921 had certainly contributed in this vein, but such an increase in bodies seemed to have little effect on symbolic wealth. The reforms initiated at the middle of the decade, by contrast, aimed to increase material resources, with more students and more courses, but they also evinced a concern with symbolic resources, through the recruitment of new student clienteles. This underscores the beliefs of the educators involved that student characteristics had an effect on subject status.

Taking the second reform first, the creation of a gender segregated course represented a reaction to the observation that commercial classes, like commercial work, had become dominated by females. A perception that this fact had negative status implications caused commercial educators throughout the continent to seek some means of redressing the balance. Many business teachers sought to model their subject on the increasingly-prestigious professional schools, which laid a heavy emphasis on masculinity; the presence of a female student body seemed to threaten this goal.[27] Of course, such concerns were unique to neither commercial studies nor North America. For instance, Brian Doyle, examining English studies in the United Kingdom, concludes: "... during the inter-war period English was ... securely established as a stable and male-dominated professional field despite the presence of a majority of female students."[28] In London, these concerns led to the decision to offer a special course to attract more young men.

In the twentieth century, the respectable and male aura of commercial studies started to diminish as more and more positions for women opened up in clerical work. The Canadian economy underwent great changes in the generation surrounding the turn of the century. A fairly sudden transformation from entrepreneurial to corporate forms of capitalism meant the volume of clerical work increased, and offices became the central directing agencies of huge economic entities. In an effort to rationalize these new phenomena, and maintain power in the hands of managers, clerical tasks became specialized and routinized. The new positions did not call for a few generalists with a wealth of skills, but for various specialists with limited skills; thus they paid poorly and offered little chance of advancement. These jobs did not suit the aspirations of most males entering the business world, but they did seem a step above traditional female paid work as a domestic or factory worker; female clerical workers flooded into the Canadian office in the first 30 years of the twentieth century.[29] By 1931, women held almost half of all clerical jobs in the country; over half of these women worked as typists and stenographers. In these junior positions, women outnumbered men by a ratio of more than twenty to one.[30]

Commercial education itself changed in reaction to these transformations. The addition of new subjects like stenography and typewriting around the turn of the century showed a curriculum adaptation to new circumstances. The commercial student body also reflected this new reality; by the time commercial education was widely and successfully established in the province, the majority of students enrolled in such courses were probably female. Young women ignored the wishes of mainstream educational reformers, who proclaimed the merits of domestic science, and eagerly sought the training which prepared them for the flood of new clerical jobs.[31] In an unpublished study, Gail Posen has found that women outnumbered men by a ratio of three to one in Toronto's High School of Commerce, from 1911 through to the Second World War.[32] In 1930, the six strictly commercial high schools operating in the province all reported a similar dominance of female students, who made up over three-quarters of the 6,721 students enrolled at those institutions.[33]

London was not immune to these provincial, national and international trends. Increasingly in the twentieth century, women took jobs in the city's clerical workforce. A comparison of the census figures for 1911 and 1921 provides a small illustration of this movement. In 1911, London's banks employed 121 male clerks and 20 female clerks, while its insurance offices employed 53 male and thirty-six female clerks. By 1921, the number of male bank clerks had increased by only one, and the number of male insurance clerks dropped by 24; over the same period, the numbers of female bank and insurance clerks increased by 81 and 82, respectively. Twenty years later, 2,393 held commercial positions in London.[34]

At the same time as women became a fixture in London's offices, their younger sisters started to change the matrix of local secondary education. From the start of the new century, girls frequently outnumbered boys at the Collegiate. Many of them ignored the domestic subjects, introduced to the local curriculum in 1902.[35] Instead they chose to take commercial studies, leading to a female dominance in the subject. Commercial studies had certainly become feminized by the time the program came to the technical school in 1920. A list of commercial diplomas awarded by the school in the first year of commercial studies included 28 female names and only six male names. In 1923 the group of students entering the first year of the commercial program numbered seventy-one females and only 19 males.[36] A similar ratio continued to mark the commercial program through the next two decades. In 1930 the number of students enrolled in commercial classes included 462 young women and 105 young men. In 1940 the school awarded 85 intermediate certificates in commercial studies, of which 70 went to young women.[37]

The possibility that this female influx had major repercussions for subject status resides in the nature of gender roles and relations at the time. In education, as in so many areas of early twentieth-century life, the experience of London's women and girls differed markedly from that of the city's men and boys. A wealth of evidence supports this interpretation at the level of the Board of Education and, especially, at the level of the teaching staff; it must have held true at the level of student.

Women in London had little representation on their Board of Education. Although one female trustee did serve a single term at the end of the nineteenth century, women only started to achieve sustained representation on the Board from 1919. Though the 1920 Board included four women out of fourteen trustees, for the next few years the board included only one or two women at a time. In 1928 the Board reduced itself to six members. The number of women members on this board stayed constant at one or two until at least 1940. Women trustees took another important step with the election of the first female Chair of the Board in 1929, followed by two more women in that office in 1933 and 1934.[38] Although the representation of women on the Board did increase over time, it never reached an equality with that of men in this period, despite the fact that both streams of feminism — maternal feminism and equal rights feminism — had an interest in education. One of these pioneer female trustees reflected the prevailing denigration of women's experience when she concluded her report of an annual convention to the Board by regretting that no male trustee from the city had attended the convention and adding: "My report is only from a woman's viewpoint."[39] The deadpan delivery of 60-year-old minutes prevents us from listening for any trace of sarcasm.

Women teachers experienced vastly different professional lives from those of their male colleagues. As in other places, London's female teachers faced discrimination in terms of status, both through official decisions on things like salaries or promotions and in the general level of treatment they received. A definite and formal gender differentiation appeared in the salaries paid teachers. As an example, the 1932 salary schedule for the London Board paid female elementary school teachers with a first class certificate a maximum of $1,800 a year, while those with a second class certificate could receive up to $1,600; the corresponding maximums for male teachers stood at $2,500 and $2,400 respectively. The terms for teachers in secondary schools were more equal, but a formal difference remained; thus teachers in the highest category received $3,400 a year if male, and $3,200 if female.[40] Of course, this latter statistic had little meaning for the majority of women teachers, clustered at the elementary level.

In terms of promotion, women could not move above the level of classroom teacher. Technically the Board did allow female principals in schools containing less than eight rooms, but in practice this meant that one teacher in each of the schools (only two operated in 1928) which had only two full-time teachers, received the title of principal, with little increase in pay or status.[41] In the secondary schools, women could not become a department head outside of the female technical subjects.[42] Advertisements for job openings always sought candidates in terms of gender; the Board ignored any women who applied for a male job unless they could find no suitable man.

One teacher recalled her experience at being hired during the Depression: "... they wanted a Commercial specialist, they wanted a man; but apparently they couldn't get a man, so they took me."[43]

Simply stated, school authorities treated female teachers as second-class employees. The Board expected women teachers who married to give up their positions, and would only consider hiring a married woman, even for a substitute position, in an emergency. When a Chair of the Board of Education spoke in favour of introducing mandatory retirement, he saw no problem in suggesting that men retire at 65 and women at 55 years of age. Of course, this all took place in a society that by and large took such things for granted. Many female teachers themselves felt it was simply logical that men have higher pay, that only men became principals, and that women should drop out when married, and turn their attention to raising a family.[44]

The creation of a special commercial course for boys in 1926, then, represented an attempt to alter the slide in subject status through the recruitment of a more socially valued student clientele; did it succeed? Did the introduction of the course actually change the gender split in the subject? The answer has to be negative. Table 1, below, outlines the gender division in new commercial students, taking all commercial courses into account, at four-year intervals. Despite the introduction of the new course in 1926, males made up roughly 20 per cent of new commercial students in 1927 and 1931, as they had in 1923. It is only in 1935 that even a minor change in ratio is detectable.

Table I.
Percentage of Students Entering First Year
of Any Commercial Course, by Gender.

	1923	1927	1931	1935
Male	21%	20%	21%	24%
Female	79%	80%	79%	76%
n=	91	325	292	406

Source: LTCHS Student Record Cards.

Despite the apparent failure of the new course to significantly alter the gender ratio in the commercial department, it still may have helped with the symbolic status of the discipline, since the mere presence of this course on the books provided evidence for commercial studies' importance. In an attempt to raise the status of commercial classes generally, the staff at Beal pointed to gender differences in education, and in particular, to the presence of young men in segregated classes. By contrast, the school did not refer to other commercial courses as being "for Girls," indicating the low status of a female clientele, and leaving the impression that all commercial courses contained some males.

While the introduction of a specifically gender segregated course reveals an obvious attempt to manipulate student characteristics, the introduction of the special one-year course demands closer inspection. In fact, the special commercial course also sought to attract a new group of students — students with a different socioeconomic background from those normally associated with the technical school. The move of the commercial department to the technical school (a result of the decrease in status associated with the gender characteristics of students) had started a further round of devaluation associated with the socioeconomic background of pupils; gender and class patterns began to interact in a vicious downward spiral. In the 1920s and 1930s, new patterns of attendance brought about by legislative and economic changes tied technical schools more and more firmly to a working class student body, perceived to have less academic ability.[45]

The composition of London's technical school's student body differed dramatically from that of the more academically-oriented Collegiate. A comparison of the occupational status of student families at the Collegiate Institute and the technical school shows this discrepancy. Table 2, below, reveals that two thirds of the pupils in the Collegiate came from families headed by men or women employed in white collar positions, while only a fifth of technical school pupils came from this group. The figures for manual occupations are reversed.

Once established at the technical school, commercial studies

Table II.
Parental Occupations, London Secondary Schools, 1922.

	C.I.	*Tech. H.S.*
Non-manual	166.3%	21.5%
Manual skilled	30.1	58.2
Manual unskilled	3.6	20.3
n=	880	423

Source: Ontario Minister of Education Annual Report (1922) pp. 228–9 and 260–61.

drew from its pool of students. Table 3, on the next page, identifies student socioeconomic status on the basis of the parental occupation listed on student record cards from the technical school. This table reveals the similarity in the socioeconomic status of students in the two general courses. The data shows that a slight difference in class characteristics of female students taking the general technical and commercial courses existed in 1927, but vanished thereafter. For 1931 and 1935, the patterns of representation seem almost identical. Thus, at least in the 1930s, class had no bearing on patterns of enrollment in the two general courses, and commercial studies thus suffered the double disability of a student body undervalued both in gender and in class terms.

The special one-year course sought to remedy this problem. Because the course demanded at least two years high school standing for admission, it enrolled only students who transferred from another secondary school, which meant in practice usually one of the Collegiate Institutes, though a few came from private schools or rural continuation schools. Many of the students entering this course had already achieved junior or senior matriculation; in a few cases, young women even attended this course after graduating from University.[46] The special commercial course thus drew students not from the general pool of students entering the technical school, but from a pool of those who had entered the Collegiate Institutes or other secondary institutions.

Table III.
Socioeconomic characteristics of female students in selected courses.

1927

	General Technical	General Commercial	Special Commercial
Non-Manual1	9%	30%	53%
Skilled Manual	40%	36%	28%
Unskilled Manual	40%	33%	19%
n=	67	129	58

1931

	General Technical	General Commercial	Special Commercial
Non-Manual	25%	24%	39%
Skilled Manual	37%	38%	42%
Unskilled Manual	38%	38%	19%
n=	92	105	69

1935

	General Technical	General Commercial	Special Commercial
Non-Manual	30%	33%	60%
Skilled Manual	33%	35%	30%
Unskilled Manual	37%	32%	10%
n=	81	135	83

Source: LTCHS Student Record Cards.

The presence of the new group of students changed the socioeconomic composition of the commercial department. Table 3 shows how the socioeconomic status of these students contrasted with that of the students in the two general courses discussed above. Where the non-manual segment of the general courses varied between a fifth and a third of all students, in the special commercial course it varied from two fifths to three fifths. At its minimum, it still exceeded the maximum for either of the other two courses.

These two new courses, then, emerged at the technical school to help raise teachers' professional status; while doing so, the courses also increased lines of segregation within the student population based on ascribed, involuntary characteristics. The creation of a course restricted to males added to the formal distinction between the genders in school society. The special one-year course produced similar, if less obvious, effects. While the new course did succeed in attracting a more highly valued clientele, in doing so it created a new division in the student body, which corresponded to a difference in socioeconomic status.

While the class-based segregation imposed by the new course did not upset proponents of social efficiency, it did mark an unintended, if acceptable, outcome. While Beal himself did attempt to minimize the social distance between the special commercial pupils and those from the general courses by organizing school-wide recreational activities,[47] these social events did nothing more than mask the systematic stratification being worked at the level of curriculum.

As is so often the case in historical research, the authors have to wonder whether their edifice of argument and evidence appears to others as little more than a house of cards. Direct evidence supports the following assertions, making them as close to "facts" as an optimistic epistemology will allow.

First, during the period 1900 to 1920, commercial studies in London, Ontario, suffered from a trend of increasing marginalization in the Collegiate Institute, which culminated in a transfer to the technical high school — an institution with a much less enviable reputation. Second, this marginalization occurred at the same time as the subject's student body underwent a process of feminization. Third, at the technical school, the commercial studies student body quickly became identical, in social class terms, to the technical student body, and different from that of the Collegiate Institute. Fourth, during 1923 and 1924 the school underwent a series of attacks led by the conservative local newspaper and city council members. Fifth, soon after these attacks ended, school officials decided to introduce two new courses which made little difference to existing students. Sixth, the first of the new courses aimed to attract C.I. students and resulted in a different class composition in the student body. Seventh, the other new course aimed at attracting males, thus directly seeking to change the student body profile.

This paper has tried to tie these seven phenomena together in one particular and specific sense by arguing for the importance of the notion of subject status. Since subject status played a major role in determining professional career status and prospects, the personal interests of commercial teachers demanded attempts to elevate the discipline's status. One way to do so involved changing the characteristics of the student body, since at this time subject status rested to a degree on the perceived value of the students enrolled. In particular, student social characteristics of gender and class acted as crucial determinants in setting the status of a particular subject. The curriculum change of the mid-1920s sought to achieve this restructuring.

In the end, the struggle for professional status resulted in a major increase in stratification and segregation in the technical school. While educators acknowledged the gender segregation, the more circumspect class segregation provided similarly potent mechanisms for structuring student experience in the school. The result was a distinction by class and gender in the credentials student received from their secondary schooling. The fact that these changes took place under provincial authority, seems to indicate that London's situation was far from unique, and might have reflected a province-wide concern with the status of commercial studies. This suggests strongly that the 1920s witnessed increased socio economic segregation in secondary school commercial courses throughout Ontario — a conclusion which matches recent interpretations of the so-called "vocational era" in the history of education.

NOTES:
1. This research was funded by a grant from the Social Sciences and Humanities Research Council of Canada. We wish to thank Ian Dowbiggin for his valuable contribution to the early stages of the Beal project.

2. Herbert M. Kliebard, *The Struggle for the American Curriculum, 1893-1958* (London: Routledge, 1986); Harvey A. Kantor, *Learning to Earn: School, Work and Vocational Reform in California, 1880–1930* (Madison: University of Wisconsin Press, 1988); David F. Labaree, T*he Making of an American High School*. (New Haven: Yale University Press, 1988). See also Janice Weiss, "The Advent of Education for Clerical Work in the High School: A Reconsideration of the Historiography of Vocationalism," *Teachers College Record*. 83 (1982): 613–638; and Jane Bernard Powers, *The 'Girl Question' in Education: Vocational Education for Young Women in the Progressive Era* (Washington: Falmer, 1992).

3. Nancy S. Jackson and Jane S. Gaskell, "White Collar Vocationalism: The Rise of Commercial Education in Ontario and British Columbia, 1870–1920," *Curriculum Inquiry*. 17 (1987): 177–202.

4. Pierre Bourdieu and Jean-Claude Passeron, *Reproduction in Education, Society and Culture*. (London: Sage, 1977); Bryan Deever, "Curriculum Change and the Process of Hegemony in an Appalachian Community," paper presented to the AERA, 1990; David F. Labaree, "Curriculum, Credentials, and the Middle Class: A Case Study of a Nineteenth-Century High School," *Sociology of Education*, 59 (1986): 42–57; Henry A. Giroux and Anthony Penna, "Social Education in the Classroom: the Dynamics of the Hidden Curriculum," in Henry Giroux and David Purpel, eds., *The Hidden Curriculum and Moral Education* (Berkeley:McCutchan, 1983); Fritz Ringer, "Introduction," in D.K. Muller, F. Ringer and B. Simon, eds., *The Rise of the Modern Educational System* (Cambridge: Cambridge University Press, 1987).

5. London, Board of Education, Advisory Vocational Committee (AVC) *Minutes*, 1922, 4. The AVC was also known as the "Industrial Advisory Committee" at one point, but for consistency this title will not be used in this paper.

6. AVC, *Minutes*, 1924, 3. Beal's comments reveal his concern with slotting students into specific occupations — a major goal of the social efficiency movement. On Beal's own commitment to social efficiency, see Ivor F. Goodson and Ian R. Dowbiggin, "Vocational Education and School Reform: The Case of the London (Canada) Technical School, 1900–1930," *History of Education Review*, 20 (1991): 39–56.

7. London, Board of Education, *Annual Report*, 1924, 77; AVC, Minutes, 1925, 3; London Technical and Commercial High School, (LTCHS) Student Record Cards, H.B. Beal Secondary School Archives; Interview with Margaret Fallona, 1990. Fallona was a student at the school in the 1920s, and a teacher in the commercial department in the 1930s.

8. AVC, *Minutes*, 1927, 7; 1928, 3.

9. See Ivor F. Goodson and Ian R. Dowbiggin, "Gender, Class, and Vocational Schooling: Technical Education for Women in London (Canada), 1870–1935," Beal Project working paper, 1989.

10. LTCHS, Student record cards; London, Board of Education, *Annual Report*, 1921, 86–88.

11. Jackson and Gaskell, "White Collar Vocationalism," 186–187.

12. J.A. Dickinson, "Commercial Education in the London Schools," in LTCHS, *The Tecalogue* (1935): 7–8; London Board of Education, *Minutes*. 1898-99: 25–26, 38, 87.

13. London, Board of Education, *Minutes*, 1899–1900: 2–3.

14. R.D. Gidney and W.P.J. Millar, *Inventing Secondary Education: The Rise of the High School in Nineteenth-Century Ontario* (Montreal: McGill-Queens University Press, 1990), 294; Jackson and Gaskell, "White Collar Vocationalism," 182–183.

15. Cited in Jackson and Gaskell, "White Collar Vocationalism," 193.

16. Ontario, Minister of Education, *Annual Report*, 1914: 84–86; 1922: 260–263.

17. London, Board of Education, *Minutes*, 1902–1915: passim.

18. London, Board of Education, *Minutes*, 1918–1919.

19. Goodson and Dowbiggin, "Vocational Education," 43–44. The best analyses of social efficiency and its effects on education can be found in Kliebard, *Struggle*, 89–122, and in Barry M. Franklin, *Building the American Community: the School Curriculum and the Search for Social Control* (Philadelphia: Falmer, 1986), 83–118.

20. AVC, Minutes, 22 January, 1918. See also London, Board of Education, *Annual Report*, 1912, 24–38.

21. Goodson and Dowbiggin, "Vocational Education and School Reform," 47–56.

22. *London Free Press*, 29 December 1923–8 February, 1924; London, Board of Education, *Minutes*, 1924: 26, 41–43.

23. London, Board of Education, *Minutes*, 1926: 350–352.

24. Fallona interview.

25. London, Board of Education, *Minutes*, 1920–21; Dickinson, "Commercial Education," p. 8.

26. This happened throughout the province, though other places did not have the excuse of a spectacular fire. See Jackson and Gaskell, "White Collar Vocationalism," 194.

27. Janice H. Weiss, "Educating for Clerical Work: A History of Commercial Education in the United States since 1850" (Ed.D., Harvard, 1978), 176–177.

28. Brian Doyle, *English and Englishness* (New York: Routledge, 1989), 71.

29. Graham S. Lowe, "Women, Work and the Office: The Feminization of Clerical Occupations in Canada, 1901–1931," in Veronica Strong-Boag and Anita Clair Fellman, eds., *Rethinking Canada: The Promise of Women's History* (Toronto: Copp Clark Pitman, 1986); Jackson and Gaskell, "White Col-

lar Vocationalism," 184–185.

30. Canada, *Census of Canada*, 1931 (v. 7), p. 74.

31. On the philosophy behind domestic science, the alternate vocational option for young women, see Diana Pedersen, "'The Scientific Training of Mothers': The Campaign for Domestic Science in Ontario Schools, 1890 - 1913," in R.A. Jarrell and A.E. Roos, eds., *Critical Issues in the History of Canadian Science, Technology and Medicine* (Thornhill: HSTC Publications, 1981) pp. 178–194; Marta Danylewycz, Nadia Fahmy-Eid and Nicole Thivierge, " L'enseignement menager et les "Home Economics" au Quebec et en Ontario au debut du 20e siecle: une analyse comparee" in J. Donald Wilson, ed., *An Imperfect Past: Education and Society in Canadian History* (Vancouver: University of British Columbia Press, 1984), 106–112; Terry Crowley, "Madonnas Before Magdalenes: Adelaide Hoodless and the Making of the Canadian Gibson Girl," *Canadian Historical Review*, 67 (1986): 520–521.

32. Gail Posen, "The Office Boom: The Relationship between the Response of the Public Education System, 1900–1940," Ontario Institute for Studies in Education, Toronto, 1980. We wish to thank Jane Gaskell for supplying us with a copy of this paper. See also, Ontario, Minister of Education, *Annual Report* (1920), 250: (1925), 216; (1930), 352.

33. Ontario, Minister of Education, *Annual Report* (1930), 352.

34. Canada, *Census of Canada* (1911) v. 6, 340, (1921) v. 4, 432–434, (1941) v. 7, 238.

35. London, Board of Education, *Minutes*, 1902–03: 5–9, 52.

36. London, Board of Education, *Annual Report*, 1921: 89; LTCHS, Student record cards. For data from 1927 and 1929, see Goodson and Dowbiggin, "Gender, Class and Vocational Schooling," 32–33.

37. Ontario, Minister of Education, *Annual Report* (1930), 353; London, Board of Education, *Annual Report*, 1940, 72–73. This feminization of commercial studies clearly took place at the expense of domestic technical subjects. In 1923 almost twice as many first year female students chose commercial studies as chose the general domestic curriculum. In later years the discrepancy grew. LTCHS, Student Record Cards; Ontario, Minister of Education, *Annual Report* (1930), 352–353; London, Board of Education, *Annual Report*, 1940, 72–73.

38. London, Board of Education, *Annual Reports*, 1898–1940.

39. London, Board of Education, *Minutes*, 1920: 93.

40. London, Board of Education, *Minutes*, 1931: appendix, n.p.

41. See London, Board of Education, *Minutes*, 1923: 43–51; 1928: 30–34.

42. London, Board of Education, *Minutes*, 1915: p. 143; Fallona interview.

43. Fallona interview; see also London, Board of Education, *Minutes*, 1921: 201.

44. London, Board of Education, *Minutes*, 1905: 95; 1933: 58; Fallona interview.

45. Jackson and Gaskell, "White Collar Vocationalism," pp. 193–194; also see Kantor, *Learning to Earn*, pp. 123–148.

46. LTCHS, Student Record Cards; Fallona interview; Interview with Pearl Morgan, 10 June, 1989. Morgan taught in the technical school at the time.

47. Morgan interview.

Chapter Three

Constructing Vocationalism
Barbara, Darlene And Me
Jane Gaskell
University of British Columbia

We have more of an instrumental, economic analysis of vocationalism than a critical and reflective sociology of it. Policy research tends to treat vocational education as a variable in the equation predicting economic outcomes. Does vocational education affect students' chances in the labour market? Does it increase economic productivity? This kind of research does not very often look inside the "black box" of vocational education to see what is going on in its name and why. Only if we understand what constitutes vocational education, however, can we hope to make sense of its effects, or to change its effects. Understanding the social processes that form vocational classrooms should be the focus of research concerned with social change and political action.

The sociology of vocationalism that has been written mostly argues that vocational classrooms reproduce the relations of subordination found in the workplace and offer working-class and minority students an inferior education. Critics of vocationalism have described vocational classes as ones where technique is reified, social control is exerted, and workers learn to accept their subordination (Bowles and Gintis, 1976; Grubb and Lazerson, 1975; Grignon, 1971). Moreover, it is argued, vocationalism serves to disadvantage working-class students by preventing their access to complex, high-status knowledge and fitting them instead with the credentials and habits of mind that ensure their continued inferiority in the workplace. It similarly separates male from female students and starts them on different and unequal trajectories into the labour market (Cockburn, 1987; Gaskell, 1992).

Both the attitudes and values that are transmitted in vocational programs and the definitions of which skills will be taught in the programs contribute to class and gender reproduction. Gleeson and Mardle (1980), in a study of the training of male mining apprentices in a British college of further education, emphasize the role of beliefs and attitudes in justifying and recreating the division of labour in the workplace through the training program. "College practice seeks to legitimate the wider social relations and conditions of work which characterize industrial life" (p. 145). "The attitudes he (the male student) learns in training are more important than the actual skills he acquires" (p. 124). Apprentice students come to the college to 'work' and are not encouraged to question their place within the relations of production or to develop critical views of either employer or college. Even the addition of "liberal studies" to the curriculum, they argue, acts only to confirm the social divisions that the training program creates and legitimizes.

Valli (1986) also looks at the role of ideology in the reproduction of gender and authority relations in a high school co-op program in clerical education. "The ideological messages the students received were fairly congruent with the gender-specific patterns and relations they had become accustomed to both in their homes and at school. In the process of elaborating their lives at work, the students utilized a fairly conventional culture of femininity which identified them not as "raw labor power", but as sex objects, on the one hand, and as office wives and mothers on the other" (p. 169). Cockburn (1987) similarly sees vocational courses as two track training, channelling young women into traditional areas of work.

Tanguay (1985) and Grignon (1971) emphasize the way definitions of skill in classrooms reproduce the existing relations of production. As Tanguay summarizes it: "the organization of production serves as a backdrop against which the techniques used in production are presented as neutral and natural facts. This exclusion of societal concerns from technical curricula leads to a neutralization of techniques and a reification of social production." Students learn how to do tasks, without reference to the reasons why, particularly as these are rooted in social, rather than technical relations: "the future worker, unaware of the why and the wherefore, learns only to use them." Tanguay argues that the increasing "scholarization" (i.e. academic location) of vocational training leads to the reduction of "practical knowledge" and absence of instruction in the "social norms of production" (p. 31) which is "displaced" to training in the company. This increased abstraction of technique from the context in which it arises further reifies the existing order.

These analyses are insightful in pointing to the processes involved in the reproduction of class and gender relations within the vocational classroom. Such accounts offer an alternative to the uncritical and optimistic ways of viewing vocational knowledge that are prevalent among vocational educators, employers and policy makers anxious for more vocational courses for "other people's children." But too often they end up portraying vocationalism as an unmitigated educational disaster, to be eliminated in favour of good old-fashioned academic education. The portrait is one-sided and mechanical, ignoring the contradictions, the possibilities for change and the resources within vocational education, both ideological and practical, which might be used to contest class and gender based orthodoxies about work and education.

We should not forget that vocational education has a history of anti-elitist politics and progressive pedagogy, at least rhetorically. John Dewey wanted more practical and vocational education in order to transform the world, not to reproduce it. He wrote in the pages of the New Republic in 1915:

> The kind of vocational education in which I am interested is not one which will "adapt" workers to the existing industrial regime; I am not sufficiently in love with the regime for that. It

seems to me that the business of all who would not be educational time-servers is to resist every move in this direction, and to strive for a kind of vocational education which will first alter the existing industrial system, and ultimately transform it (quoted in Drost, 1977).

At the turn of the century, women's groups and labour unions supported reforms which would add vocational courses — home economics, industrial education, technical education and typing — to the school curriculum. They saw vocationalism as an alternative to the existing elitist and male dominated curriculum, an alternative which might shake up the schools, include more working-class students, increase the respect given to women's work and break down the barriers between mental and manual, theory and practice. For example, in 1913, Albert Leake, director of technical education in Ontario, advocated vocationalism in order to keep more students in school, and away from the "physical and moral degradation caused by work which provides neither education in the present nor economic prospects for the future" (p. 19: 1913). He rejected the inscription of class distinctions in curriculum through the separation of vocational and liberal education, and quotes Ruskin: "We are always in these days endeavoring to separate intellect and manual labor; we want one man to be always thinking and another working, and we call one a gentleman and the other an operative; whereas the workman ought often to be thinking and the thinker ought often to be working, and both should be gentlemen in the best sense" (p. 20). His aims for industrial education included "the education of both the parent and the boy with a view of showing them that continued education is worth while, materially, morally, and spiritually, and the inculcation of the idea that industrial occupations are to be desired and sought rather than shunned" (p. 39). The needs of industry mattered to him, but his image was certainly not of deskilled education without intellectual and ethical content.

Leake did not find the vocational needs of girls of much interest, but women's groups at the time also saw vocationalism harnessed to reform, equality and progress (Powers, 1992). While there was much debate about the forms that vocational education should take to increase equality for girls and women, many saw vocational education as a way to prepare women to move outside the home into new roles involving paid labour. Others saw the development and elaboration of vocational education for women's traditional work in the home as a new recognition of its complexity and value.

Gleeson (1989), reflecting on recent vocational initiatives in Britain, comments on ways that progressive pedagogy continues as part of the vocational tradition. He finds that what he calls "prevocational" classes "explore experimental pedagogies, involve greater student participation and advocate active learning strategies" (p. 65). Spours and Young (1988), also in the British context, develop proposals for the integration of work education and liberal education in ways that improve both. Simon, Dippo and Schenke (1991) work in a similar tradition in the Canadian context, developing curricula which use vocationalism to challenge the taken-for-granteds of working life, of power, racism, class and gender.

Analysis of vocational classrooms needs to be sensitive to the possibilities of 'counterhegemonic' education, as well as to the possibilities of reproducing traditional divisions. There are reasons why the ideology of the classroom is likely to reflect the employer's viewpoint (as it is conceived by instructors, sociologists or students) and the skills taught and learned are likely to be decontextualized and reified, but there is nothing mechanical about the process. It is worked out by instructors, by curriculum committees, and in the classroom with students. Vocational classes are sometimes open to workers' concerns and instructors do not always identify wittingly or unwittingly with the interests of capital and patriarchy. Vocational classes are filled with both instructors and students who have extensive knowledge of the workplace, and much of this knowledge comes from experience in non-management positions.

Seeing vocational classrooms as places where knowledge, representations of the workplace and definitions of skill are contested is more likely to inform vocational instruction than seeing them as sites for the imposition of class and gender privilege. For the definition of vocational curriculum is constructed and contingent. As Page and Valli (1990) put it, curriculum differentiation is a "provisional, recursive, interactive process of negotiation, rather than a universal, final, tidy solution" (p. 232). Arguments that vocational knowledge is or is not worth teaching, should or should not be continued, stopped or increased are too simplistic. We need to understand more about what does goes on in the name of vocationalism, and how we might encourage a more critical and contextual exploration of working knowledge. We need to understand more about the contexts which shape vocational curriculum, and the understandings, cultures and structural processes that mediate it.

In this paper, I explore the varying constructions of the meaning of vocational education for instructors in two public community college programs that train secretaries. Both programs are based in the Vancouver area. Both admit students who have completed secondary school and want further clerical training in typing, shorthand, dictatyping, word processing, office procedures and business communication. The colleges offer specialized programs for legal and medical secretaries, as well as general programs in office work. There are virtually no men enrolled as students in either program, and only three of the 29 instructors interviewed were men. At each college, the programs have an advisory committee of employers who help ensure the curriculum prepares students for the workplace.

I concentrate here on the views of two instructors, Barbara and Darlene, who were articulate, energetic and quite different in their approaches to teaching. They made me reflect further on why they said what they said about their students, the curriculum and their relations to the workplace. This paper explores only talk about vocationalism, leaving out questions of what actually happens in classrooms and what institutional processes affect it. My purpose is to emphasize the contradictions and difficulties within constructions of vocationalism, and to begin to explore these constructions in a more nuanced way. For these constructions not just personal idiosyncrasies and preferences; they matter for students, for the workplace, for all of us.

Barbara And Darlene: Two Views

Both Barbara and Darlene are 'good' teachers, hardworking, concerned about their students, up to date in their fields. Both have worked as secretaries, are university educated and in their late thirties. Both are concerned to produce better opportunities for women in the workplace, but they have very different views of what this means in the classroom.

Barbara starts the interview by explaining how important it is for her to keep in close touch with employers in order to meet their needs more exactly:

> If you can match the students to the firms, you keep the firms happy. That then enhances the program ... by putting a good student out, they (employers) are happy and they'll come back again. They will tell their friends and their friends tell their friends. That's the way it works. In this way we keep our own program marketable.... My program will crunch if I don't get the support of the business community.

She is proud of her good relationship with employers and spends a lot of time on the phone to them keeping up contacts, finding out what's going on, and placing her students. She explains the advantage to employers: "If a firm that I am in contact with phones me up, they don't want to go through agencies and have to pay. They don't want to go through the newspaper and have 200 applicants they have to screen. So it pays them." The advantage to her, the college and the students is that her students find employment when they graduate, a fact that makes the program attractive to students, to the government which is looking at placement rates to make decisions about where to purchase places, and to college administrators who need to show the demand for their programs.

The consequence of her need to please employers is pressure to turn out students who will meet employers' requirements. "If I tried to foist a student off to a firm who isn't up to par, I am only going to get it in the back of the neck...." So Barbara screens her students with the eyes of an employer, and works hard to make them acceptable to the best employers. She feels personally accountable for her students, as she explains in relation to one student whom she sees as marginal: "If she doesn't work out, I'm going to bury my head."

Barbara's identification with employers leads her to emphasize productivity, working under pressure and immediate responsiveness to the employer's demands in her classroom. "I'll do terrible things like I'll wait for a student to get half way through a document and tell them take that out of your typewriter. I want you to go back and correct this. The first time I did it the student looks at me and sort of stands up. 'Oh, no. I'm not going to do it. How am I going to get it back in?' You've got to do these kinds of horrible little things to simulate what it is really like in an office."

Her classroom is experienced as a pressure cooker by students, but she justifies it. "If they can't start to work on their own and they can't start to figure things out, use their initiative and common sense, they are just going to be flops working." She tries to simulate the world of the office in her classroom, and in the process reproduces many of the things her students, and workers in general, hate in the workplace. She wants to accustom students to having little control and little authority, so they become docile and obedient workers, and get hired:

> This is a very large onus put on a student. I think it has built up maturity in the students, it has built up responsibility. It has made them realize that deadlines have to be met. If you don't meet a deadline you are going to lose a grade for doing it. They are at the productivity that is required to start working. I assume you know that some firms are sweat shops.

She stresses skills, and materials that are "up-to-date." She wants the forms that are currently in use in law firms; so students can learn to fill them in. "If I have no rapport with the legal field, I can't keep my materials up to date. I can't do anything for the students.... It would be like taking a student out to the edge of the cliff and saying, okay, 10,000 feet, and they drop off the end."

She thinks basic math and English skills are critical to success at work, but does not conclude that she should teach them. She sees her program as standing between general schooling and the employers. "High schools need to get their proverbial act together" in relation to mathematics and literacy, for these are basic to doing secretarial work. She believes students who do not have this level of proficiency should not be admitted to her program. "We cannot take a 19- or a 23- or a 38-year-old and teach them English or teach them math in three months or two months. I think the whole thing is a complete sham. The high schools have got to be responsible for educating, certainly in math and English." And, she says, students from other countries or students who need high school equivalence should go to adult upgrading programs. "I'm looking at things from a realistic point of view. We are faced with budget crunches, we are faced with the situation whereby we have got to get people out into the work force as quickly as we possibly can. If we don't have the money we can't spend the time. You've got to cut the corners somewhere."

Appearance and attitudes are high on Barb's list of what matters to employers. "Last week someone phoned me up and said, 'Barb, I need somebody and she's going to have to be good looking,' and I went 'Oh!' I mean they say these things to me that they would not say to a lot of other people because it is against all human rights and the rest of it." But, knowing the importance of dress in the workplace, Barbara emphasizes it at the college. "I tell them basically what to wear.... Isn't that awful? But I do." She describes the students who will not get a job: "She had a disgusting attitude, she dressed poorly and her attitude was obnoxious. She has dress problems.... Her hair sticks out like this, she looks like the Wild Woman of the West, she is not going to get a job, it's as easy as that. Forget it. She isn't even going to be looked at for 20 seconds." These students become a problem because they may pass the tests, but they are not acceptable to employers and she must not have her program identified with them. Barbara experiences these conflicts personally: "I've got the firm here and I've got the college here.... I'm in an awkward situation, I feel I'm not really being an employee of the college sometimes."

By identifying so completely with the employers, she feels she serves students well, but understands that she pushes the limits of college rules. "I find those students who are prepared to work hard then I'm prepared to hustle my butt at the end for them. I'm sure there is a certain amount of favouritism there, but I guess I'm trying to save my own butt in the long run."

Barbara identifies closely with employers and frames her curriculum from their point of view, as she understands it. She also feels constrained by the space and time available for instruction, and relies on screening to keep some students out of her program. For the rest, she tries to produce in her classroom an environment that simulates the workplace, and to judge her students with employers' eyes. She feels personally responsible for placing her students, and feels she can serve them best by maintaining a good relationship with the firms who might employ them. This involves rewarding in her classroom the class and gender relations that employers prefer — docility, hard work and traditional femininity. It means screening students on criteria that are used by employers, and sometimes ignoring "that human rights stuff" or the needs of students as workers. She tries to help her students get ahead at work; she wants them to do better than students from other colleges or training programs.

An alternative view is presented by Darlene. She feels that the college identifies too much with the point of view of employers, and she wants the curriculum to respond more closely to the needs of students, and ultimately to their needs as workers. She expresses her views as opposition to the dominant mode at the college:

> I don't believe that the college's responsibility is to turn out workers who will be able to be re-plugged in on the fifth floor of the Bentall Centre (a downtown office block). [The employers] description of what a student would need to know is based on their point of view of standing in their office wanting to get more work done faster for less.... I think they are looking for a person who will almost come ready made so it makes their interviewing easier ... like they can measure them up on the wall and see if they are exactly the right shape and it can completely absolve them of the responsibility for ongoing training in that person's working life. That makes me angry. I think it is their responsibility.... We are not trying to train them to fit into a job that someone describes at a particular location, unless the person guarantees that the job will be there when your student has completed and unless the student has some aptitude and interest in that job.

Instead of emphasizing the specific skills and attitudes that employers want, Darlene wants to emphasize "understanding" and the students' ability to stand up for themselves. Part of the reason she gives for this is that no one knows what specific skills will in fact be required:

> I'd like to drown (Mr. X) every time he comes out with those outrageous statements like 'there won't be any unions in the future' and 'everyone will be a self-contractor and work from home.' Like no one knows that. I still have great faith in the necessity in your life to be a flexible, generally well educated person, just educated person, just so you can cope with whatever is happening. So it worries me that the college programs get too specific. I think the training is short sighted in so far as it emphasizes machine applications, distinct from decision making a citizen would be involved in in order to effect the full use of the equipment. Why word processing is here and how you as an employee use the word processing have an influence over your work life, but it is not discussed.

Unlike Barbara, she is unhappy with the ways that the college simulates the workplace:

> I feel like the supervisor of a word processing facility rather than a teacher in a classroom; the tremendous amount of stuff the students have to go through. The lecture time, the students go prepared to hear me but they don't go prepared to enter into any kind of conversation or express opinions about what's happening to their lives. They have commented that that is a bit of a shock that I ask so many questions. I expect them to have done a certain amount of reading in their textbook. For instance, today I was to lecture on reprographics — copying and duplicating — and I walked in and the first thing I said was, 'what's the most common kind of duplicating technology available in most offices?', and they alwaysgiggle. They expect that I am there to provide the information and they open up their books and write down what I say and then I don't say anything. I ask them what do you think? And then they laugh. We were talking about the advantages and disadvantages of different technologies and I asked them what were the disadvantages of photocopying. No one had any thought about why authors might not want their material to be photocopied and how that would affect their livelihood. And, then finally one of the students said, 'That's against the law isn't it, to copy a book without the permission of the author?' And I said, 'Raise your hand in this class if you haven't ever photocopied a book without the permission of the author.' And they all laughed again. But they don't expect to come here and make any of these kinds of con-

nections in their lives, they just ... let me work away on the keyboard and let me take these notes. They are ready to go at this frantic pace for a full three months and then go out into the world and do that again in their jobs without having made any decisions.

For Darlene technology increases the necessity for students to be thoughtful:

> As soon as you get out there the technology will change so the most important thing for you to know is what values you are looking for in order to make a reasonable decision. In your career you will at some point be the person who will be consulted to make the decision. I want them to look at these things here, that decision-making is going to be part of their work as well. I guess I secretly hope that if I plant enough of those ideas that they will agitate for the right to make those decisions, rather than just accepting.

Darlene takes up feminist issues in class, encouraging students to take their careers seriously, and discussing the devaluation of women's work. She talks about issues in the workplace, safety standards and ergonomics. She sees dress as an issue to be "discussed" in class and "negotiated" between employer and worker. She tries to get students to take their own needs seriously, and hopes that in doing so they may help to change the workplace. She talks about the dilemmas this poses, not wanting to "take the responsibility of making students feel that they ought to stick up for their rights in a way that might just put them right out of the job market altogether." But, ultimately she wants to help her students by encouraging them to transform the nature of secretarial work.

These two instructors identify what is needed in the workplace quite differently. Barbara wants to meet what she understands as the immediate needs of employers, for the welfare of her students and for the welfare of the program. She wants to please employers by doing for them what they might otherwise have to do themselves — screening applicants and training them very specifically for entry level jobs. Darlene wants to meet the needs of students by preparing them for a workplace which she construes as needing more general skills and thoughtfulness, and ultimately by increasing the control workers exercise in the workplace. She wants them to stand up for their rights, and assumes employers will hire them if they are competent at the work. In the process of carrying through their versions of an appropriate curriculum, both Barbara and Darlene translate their own views of appropriate class and gender relations into a vision of what they should be doing in the classroom.

They are different politically, in what they value, how they see themselves and whose point of view they adopt. But they are also different in their assessments of where different kinds of education should take place, and in their descriptions of what employers and students 'really' need. Their accounts of how the world works, as well as their values, lie behind curriculum decisions. A vocational teacher in a 'business' program must concern herself with preparing students for office jobs. Her views of what office jobs are like, her views of the capacities and interests of her students and her assessment of employers' responsibilities and interests all inform her account of what this entails.

Contesting The Taken-For-Granted: Whose Construction Of Skills?

The need to make students employable shapes vocational curriculum, almost by definition. Students' 'employability' dominates curriculum discourse, but its meaning is constructed. Does it mean getting a job or coping with work once one is employed. What kinds of knowledge and skills and beliefs and attitudes does it entail? Given that there are differences out there in the business world, which workplaces are used as the model of what is required? This is the discussion that has been hidden in the staff rooms and the one that needs to be understood and joined by analysts and policy makers. It is here that instructors' taken-for-granted constructions of the world can be debated and held up for critical scrutiny.

Instructors, by the nature of their work, are at some distance from the settings where their students will be employed. They get information about changing job requirements formally through advisory committees, informally through friends, through their own previous experiences as office workers, through professional journals, visits to employers, and feedback from students who have found jobs. Occasionally teachers will do more formal surveys of employers and journals will publish systematic data on what is 'really' needed at work. Occasionally advisory committees will be very forceful and ensure a particular pattern is adopted. There is a good deal of literature in business education trying to construct accurately what clerical jobs do require so that instructors can be better informed in the way they carry out their courses.

This kind of enterprise assumes that there is one notion of what clerical jobs entail, and that the problem is simply getting at it more accurately. It ignores the way that any version of skill requirements is socially constructed, and interested (Gaskell, 1992). Different people, with different relationships to the work will describe it in different ways. Political struggles over job classifications, the relative value of the work, and its educational needs, reflect different accounts of what the work is like.

Moreover, the number of jobs for which any particular student might apply is very large, and the variability among jobs means that the curriculum must focus on some jobs rather than others, or abstract only what seems common to them all, which might not be very much at all. Entry level jobs require less than jobs workers might be promoted into through internal labour markets. Instructors, collectively and/or individually, in deciding on a vocational curriculum, develop an account of what kind of preparation for work they will provide themselves, and what kind of preparation should be provided elsewhere. They decide how many and what kinds of people can be trained for work, what is necessary in the way of previous education, personality, language, and self presentation in order to be admitted. They make some judgements about what can be effectively taught before job entry, and what is better learned on the job. This involves questions of effectiveness (what will students remember and use) and political questions about what employers should be obliged to pay for in the way of training their workers, and what should be taught at the expense of the student or the state.

But most importantly, instructors must decide from whose point of view they will assess what is needed in the workplace.

What is 'needed' by the employer to get the work done faster, is different from what is 'needed' by the worker herself to ensure her indispensability and to feel in control of the work process. What women need to cope with sexual harassment and take advantage of promotion opportunities is different from what men need to preserve their privileged access to power. Each of these accounts of what is needed might be different again from what is needed by the consumer of the services that are produced by the company. Whose needs count?

There is no single answer in the community of vocational educators. There is no single answer in the either of the programs I looked at. There are competing discourses, and cultural and structural resources can be amassed for many views, even in programs which seem coherently marshalled around an agreed upon set of courses and requirements. Identification with the employer and identification with the student/worker coexist in an uneasy relation in any educational program. There are structural pressures encouraging instructors to take the point of view of the employers. They need the support of the business community. They need to find jobs for their students. They need to convince the government that there is a demand for their skills, their knowledge, their graduates. Many of the instructors have been supervisors or employers of clerical workers, and they identify with the problems of management.

On the other hand, there are structural factors that encourage instructors to take the point of view of their students, and of workers. Instructors are hired to educate, to help students learn and ultimately lead more satisfying lives. Vocational instructors in clerical programs have often worked as secretaries themselves. They are in close contact with students, and easily empathize with their problems and frustrations. They also have an interest in upgrading the status of the occupation, a status which they come to share as instructors. There are organizational forms and a culture here which could support a more transformative vocationalism.

In the literature I referred to at the beginning of this essay, reproduction in vocational classrooms was linked to ideology and to the social construction of skill. But instructors' constructions of 'attitudes' (i.e. ideology) and 'content' (i.e. skills) are contested by the instructors in these two programs. What becomes critical is how the different accounts are taken up by the institutions within which the instructors are located.

It is not hard to describe ways in which instructors' talk leads to the reproduction of the workplace in their classes. Students are being made 'employable.' Employers do the hiring. It is not surprising to see an emphasis on individual mobility and "the business point of view." But rather than leaving it at that, it is important to find the spaces where dialogue takes place, where difference exists and disagreement over the character of appropriate knowledge is expressed. There is room in vocational programs for instructors' advocacy for their students as workers. There are instructors who identify with the occupation and with their students and want a better deal for both. Training is a site for struggle, just as the workplace is, and as educators we need to open up these spaces further.

Vocational education is as diverse and variable as education that is not labelled vocational. While the immediate context of the workplace gives employers' views great prominence, the immediate context of the workplace also makes the perspective of workers more prominent. In female jobs where skills have been undervalued, revaluing them has some positive features. While it is clear that the possession of specialized and esoteric skills in itself does not guarantee power and status — shorthand never did secretaries much good — the notion of pride in craft, of the importance and value of secretarial skills, seems a prerequisite for political demands to enhance the power and perceived value of the occupation. It is important to go beyond blanket statements about vocational education to an examination of differences among settings. It is important to go beyond research that treats instructors as "cultural dopes," to research that treats them as active participants in the making of vocational knowledge.

References

Bowles, Sam and Gintis, Herbert, *Schooling in Capitalist America: Educational Reform and the Contradictions of Economic Life*. New York: Basic Books, 1976.

Cockburn, Cynthia, *Two Track Training: Sex Inequalities and the YTS.* London: Macmillan Education Ltd, 1987.

Davies, Marjorie, *Woman's Place is At the Typewriter: Office Work and Office Workers 1870-1930.* Philadelphia: Temple University Press, 1983.

Drost, Walter, "Social Efficiency Reexamined: The Dewey-Sneddon Controversy," *Curriculum Inquiry*, 7:1 (1977): pp. 19–32.

Gaskell, Jane, *Gender Matters from School to Work.* Milton Keynes: Open University Press, 1992.

Gleeson, Dennis and Mardle, G., *Further Education or Training?* London: Routledge and Kegan Paul, 1980.

Gleeson, Dennis, *The Paradox of Training.* Milton Keynes: Open University Press, 1989.

Grignon, Claude, *L'Ordre des Choses: Les Fonctions sociales de l'enseignement technique.* Paris: Minuit, 1971.

Grubb, Norton and Lazerson, Marvin, "Rally Round the Workplace: Continuities and Fallacies in Career Education," *Harvard Educational Review*, 45 (1975): pp. 451–474.

Leake, Albert, *Industrial Education: Its Problems Methods and Dangers.* Boston: Houghton Mifflin, 1913.

Melosh, Barbara, *The Physician's Hand Work, Culture and Conflict in American Nursing.* Philadelphia: Temple University Press, 1982.

Oakes, Jeannie, *Keeping Track: How Schools Structure Inequality.* New Haven: Yale University Press, 1985.

Page, Reba and Valli, Linda, *Curriculum Differentiation: Interpretive Studies in U.S. Secondary Schools.* Albany: SUNY Press, 1990.

Powers, Jane Bernard, *The Girl Question in Education: Vocational Education for Young Women in the Progressive Era.* London: Falmer Press, 1992.

Simon, Roger, "But Who Will Let You Do It? Counter Hegemonic Possibilities for Work Education," *Journal of Education* 165:3 (1983): pp. 235–256.

Simon Roger, Dippo, Don and Schenke, Arlene, *Learning Work.* New York: Bergin and Garvey, 1991.

Spours, Ken and Young, Michael F. D., *Beyond Vocationalism: A New Perspective on the Relationship Between Work and Education.* Institute of Education Post 16 Education Centre, Working Paper No. 7, 1988.

Tanguay, Lucie, "Academic Studies and Technical Education: New Dimensions in an Old Struggle in the Division of Knowledge," *Sociology of Education*, 58:1 (1985): pp. 20–33.

Valli, Linda, *Becoming Clerical Workers.* Boston: Routledge and Kegan Paul, 1986.

Chapter Four

Schooling, Work And Life
Reflections Of The Young In The 1940s

Rebecca Priegert Coulter
University of Western Ontario

Policy debates about the transition from school to work have occurred in Canada for more than a century now. However, in periods of economic crisis or restructuring when Canadian business fears for its international competitiveness or market share and workers fear for their jobs, these debates intensify and education, especially the schooling of the young, often becomes both the scapegoat and the solution.[1] And, as adults, whether industrialists or unionists, politicians or teachers, try to make sense of and shape their economic and social world through education-based solutions, what is often lost is any sense of how young people themselves experience and understand school-work linkages and make efforts to improve their own life circumstances. For historians analyzing how education has been used both to explain unemployment and economic downturns and to provide hope for improvement and economic renewal, the absence of the voices of youth is particularly problematic.

In the context of Canadian history, however, there are a

small number of specific moments when young people have had opportunities to speak out about their concerns.[2] Such a time occurred during the 1940s when the Canadian Youth Commission (CYC) was established as an independent organization for the purposes of studying the problems of young people between the ages of 15 and 24 and making recommendations for measures to accommodate the needs of the young after the war.

The CYC conducted both quantitative research through means such as a national survey conducted by the Canadian Institute of Public Opinion and qualitative research through in-depth ("intensive") interviews with young people in all the provinces and with those serving with the armed forces overseas. In addition, the CYC developed what must be an early model of action research by gathering young people in study groups, meetings and provincial conferences across the country to consider prepared study materials, make recommendations, write briefs and organize themselves for further study and activities.[3] The results of the work of the CYC provide a rich source for historians wanting to analyze the ways in which young people themselves understood the social relations of schooling and work.

When the CYC began its national survey in 1943, it did so at a time when young people had been through the desperation of the Depression and were living the searing experiences of a world war. In particular, most of the youths in the upper half of the 15 to 24-year-old age cohort would have developed a concrete and personal understanding of youth unemployment as they searched for work in the latter part of the 1930s. Likely, they also learned about the inability of a youth training scheme, the Dominion-Provincial Youth Training Programme, to make any significant contribution to the securing of employment.[4] With the outbreak of war in 1939, however, the economic tables turned and work was available for most young people who wanted it. Indeed, by the time the CYC began its research, adults were complaining that too many young people had taken on war work to the detriment of high school program completion.

In fact, an interesting shift in adult opinions about youth can be observed over the course of about 10 years. In the 1930s social commentaries focused on the debilitating effects of unemployment. Fears were expressed about the increasing dependency of youth, about the loss of skills, fitness and morale resulting from unemployment, about sexual promiscuity and the climbing rates of illegitimate births which were attributed to the economic necessity of delayed marriage, about declining standards of morality and higher rates of juvenile crime and about the incursion of subversive doctrines among the ranks of the idle young. Admittedly, most of the concern was reserved for the problems of young men for it was believed that young women were less vulnerable to unemployment as they could always be "absorbed" by working in their family homes or in the homes of others.[5] Education and training were seen in terms of increasing the employability of the young and were often discussed in the language of hospitals and prisons. Training became "rehabilitation" for young people with all that implies about personal disabilities and individual solutions.[6]

By the early 1940s youth unemployment and dependency ceased to be a worry and the focus of concern shifted to the independence young people enjoyed as a result of being able to earn wages at an early age. While many young people received training in skilled work through War Emergency Training Programmes, there was a growing fear that young, people were sacrificing schooling for the short-term gain of war work in "blind alley occupations." There was, however, a continuity of concern about delinquency among the young though now it was because they had "money to burn." Youthful sexuality, especially that of girls whose ability to support themselves made it possible for them to evade the constant supervision of parents, also troubled many adults.[7]

It is in this social context that the CYC began its national survey of the opinions of the young. While the idea of the CYC had originated with the YMCA and the American Youth Commission offered a model for its Canadian cousin to consider, it remains true that the CYC was very much an autonomous and Canadian organization. The Commission itself had 54 members, seven of whom were women, chosen to represent Canada's regions, linguistic groups and the Roman Catholic, Protestant and Jewish faiths. Among them, the commissioners represented a wide range of interests including government, business, unions, churches and the farm community. Individuals also were selected for the other contacts and networks they would bring with them. For example, the CYC was chaired by Sidney Smith who was president of the University of Manitóba and who in 1945 became president of the University of Toronto. One of the co-chairs was Hugh Keenleyside from the Department of External Affairs and the other was Senator Leon-Mercier Gouin. The daily work of the CYC was guided by a hired director, R.E.G. ("Dick") Davis and associate director, George Tuttle, who were supported by a small staff and the unpaid work of Margaret Davis, the wife of the director.[8]

The CYC was concerned to explore many aspects of the lives of young people and addressed topics such as youth and the family, youth and religion, youth and recreation, youth and health, youth and education and youth and jobs. Separate national committees, each chaired by a member of the Commission, were set up to oversee the research and other work related to each topic. Members of the committees were co-opted by the chair from within his/her network and the expertise of other members of the Commission was utilized in an advisory capacity.[9]

Two committees are of particular relevance for a consideration of schooling and work, namely the Committee on Education and the Committee on Youth Employment. The culmination of the work of these two committees is represented in two published volumes, *Youth and Jobs in Canada* and *Youth Challenges the Educators*,[10] but the working files of the committees provide fascinating evidence about the thoughts and feelings young people harboured about school curriculum and experiences and about the preparation of the young for paid and unpaid work.

Young people's views were gathered in four different ways. The Canadian Institute of Public Opinion was commissioned to conduct a national survey of youth opinion. A total of 1,444 young Canadians, 840 women and 579 men, responded to a series of questions about a wide range of topics including aspects of schooling, work, religious beliefs, politics and the economy. The sampling was done carefully in order to ensure appropriate representation from the regions, from persons of upper, middle and lower income groups, from various religious groups, from rural areas and from small, medium and large centres of population, from both sexes and from those both in school and out of school.[11] A second survey of 1,467 young people, 756 women and 711 men, was conducted by the CYC's Committee on Education with the purpose of specifically and carefully probing what young people thought of their education.[12]

To supplement the data gathered through the questionnaire surveys the CYC developed a system to conduct 200 intensive interviews with a representative sample of young people from each province. However, limited financial resources meant that the CYC had to use volunteers to organize its work in the regions and conduct the interviews. Most of these volunteers appear to have been recruited from the middle class and this may have biased the choice of interviewees and the ways in which questions were asked and interview data recorded. Nonetheless, the interview questions were open-ended, and while adults may have been selective in what they wrote down, what they did record was often enough in words young people themselves would have used.[13]

The fourth and final source of data was the 800 briefs received from various youth groups and from the youth conferences held in many different centres. The final report on youth and employment observed that these briefs "represent[ed] the voice of organized youth, socially conscious, articulate young people, who have cultivated the means to speak and be heard."[14] Many briefs came from small groups such as local church youth clubs but many others came from much larger organizations or delegate conferences. The Calgary Youth Conference, for example, was attended by about 600 young people, most of whom came as delegates from about 50 youth organizations.[15] The Winnipeg Youth Conference was attended by 306 delegates, 54 of whom represented church groups and 72 of whom represented student groups at high schools, universities and nursing schools. The rest of the youth delegates came from a range of locations including the unions (27), service clubs (29) and ethnic organizations (35).[16] From this evidence it might be concluded that the CYC solicited and received opinions from a very wide and open range of young people through provincial conferences.

Some caution needs to be exercised in reaching an uncritical conclusion about the diversity of opinions gathered. The CYC did much of its work through a framework of provincial and municipal committees, members of which were volunteers. These volunteers were in many ways the successors to the Canadian child savers, those mostly middle-class social reformers whose work in organizing public health and welfare agencies, youth groups, vocational education, supervised playgrounds and the juvenile justice system has been well-described by social historians.[17] Persons committed to and doing the work of the CYC, then, came to their tasks with a particular kind of reformist agenda which had historical antecedents. In important senses, the CYC was a political and organizational strategy for expanding earlier forms of youth work.

The CYC's work in Alberta provides an example of this. The provincial committee was chaired by Reg Rose who, when he began as chair, was the administrator of the Edmonton Community Chest, a precursor of the United Way.[18] Local (municipal) organizations of volunteer adults-ministers, church and youth workers, teachers, professors, lawyers, and civil servants were established in Edmonton and Calgary under the umbrella of the provincial committee. In Edmonton the local group was called the Advisory Youth Commission Committee. It was established in February, 1944 for the purpose of organizing a committee of young people.

Although there appear to be no records to confirm this, it is likely that members of the youth committee were chosen from already established youth groups deemed to be 'suitable' by the adults of the Advisory Committee. Certainly there is other evidence to suggest that adults were interested in exercising some control over the activities of youth involved with the CYC. In 1945, for example, George Tuttle wrote the General Secretary of the Edmonton YMCA inquiring in confidence about the possibility of the local youth committee joining a new youth federation headed by some 'progressive' youth leaders. The letter clearly suggests that there might be a problem for the CYC if youth groups currently associated with the CYC joined this new federation of youth. The somewhat conspiratorial tone of the correspondence implies an understanding between the author and the recipient that certain forms of youth activity would have to be monitored and controlled in a quiet and unobtrusive way.[19]

In Calgary, the local committee was chaired by Father Patrick O'Byrne, a Roman Catholic priest.[20] The all-adult membership of the committee was drawn from eleven Protestant denominations, Mount Royal College, the Calgary Normal School, the YMCA, the YWCA, the Council of Social Agencies, the City of Calgary Child Welfare Department, the high schools, the Alberta Department of Education and labour groups.[21] It is also clear that some groups were carefully excluded from participation, namely political parties and groups that had any affiliation with the Canadian Youth Congress, a progressive, left-leaning young people's organization.[22] Thus, despite the claim of R.E.G. Davis that "we are consulting youth directly and finding out what youth itself thinks, not what adults think youth thinks,"[23] adults were deciding what would count as 'acceptable' youth opinion.

Adults also structured the discourse in another way. In Edmonton, the adult Advisory Committee allowed the 16-member youth committee it had struck to plan a three-evening conference. This conference was attended by 102 young people[24] who heard speakers such as the Hon. Mr. Justice O'Connor; Dr. M.E. Lazerte, dean of the Faculty of Education, University of Alberta and Abe Miller, a prominent Edmonton lawyer, in workshop sessions organized around themes such as "Youth and Work Opportunities," "Youth and Education," and "Youth and Citizenship."[25] The preliminary report of this conference shows the considerable role the 'experts' played in setting the appropriate topics for discussion and in structuring the discussions themselves. At the same time, youth delegates were urged to take the suggestions in the published conference report back to their respective youth groups for further discussion. As the program chair said to the delegates, "No statement made in it [the conference report] is final — it is for you and your discussion group to discuss, investigate and bring in well thought-out recommendations."[26] In fact, some youths found the CYC-initiated discussions and conference so positive, they established a co-ordinating, independent youth organization in the city to foster further study of problems pertaining to the welfare of Canada.[27]

While caution must be exercised, it seems reasonable to think that, taken together and read in comparative ways which allow for cross-checking, the two national surveys, the intensive interviews and the briefs provide at least a partial picture of the ways in which young people experienced, understood and made their way in the world. Certainly, the intensive interviews have a ring of authenticity about them against which we can read the national surveys and the briefs from youth organizations and conferences.

On February 20, 1945, Henry F. Hall, a well-known social worker in Montreal, interviewed a 26-year-old, French-Canadian woman who had completed high school and a course in business college.[28] She was the daughter of a train conductor and was working as a secretary and attending an evening college. Of her earlier education she had this to say: "My past education was not at all a training necessary for a person who wishes to face the problems of life and of society...[. I]t did not help me to choose a life work nor to prepare for it." She was determined to become a physician ("I will not let anything stand in the way!") and that was why she was attending evening college. When asked whether she believed she could have both a career and a marriage, she responded, "I feel that I want both and would not like to give up one for the other. I feel, however, that one must always pay a price for any great thing and perhaps this [i.e. no husband] is it."

When asked for her views on what was needed to improve life in Canada for the young, she named improvements in education and social security. She noted that we live in "a big business country" and "some individual leaders forget people's welfare in the search for profit." When pressed on her position about social security measures and asked whether such measures might not lead to a loss of individual freedom, she replied, "On the contrary, security is the only thing that can bring freedom to the majority — that and education — real education." The women of French Canada, she went on to say, were in real need of help and leadership of various kinds.

Henry Hall clearly was impressed with Marie. On the bottom of the interview transcript, he wrote a comment praising her but wondering whether she was perhaps an atypical young person. However, he concluded with the observation that "her type may be commoner than many people would think." In fact, while Marie's discussion of the purposes of education, her understanding of gender issues and her positive attitude towards state intervention in the economy were expressed in relatively sophisticated ways, her views were more or less shared by a substantial majority of young Canadians. In the national youth opinion poll, 62% of the 1,444 young people surveyed said they would "like to see many changes or reforms made in Canada." Fully 81% supported government intervention in the economy with respect to ensuring full employment after the war and 50% were willing to support a post-war continuation of wartime controls on business and industry.

Less than half (46%) of the young people who had already left high school thought schools were doing a good job of teaching people how to make a living, though 51% thought the schools did a good job in guiding people to choose suitable occupations. In contrast, only 18% felt that the schools were successful in preparing people for marriage and family life. Forty-two per cent of the young people out of school indicated that they had to leave because they were financially unable to continue and 92% believed that "the government should make it possible for all young people who have the ability, but not the money, to go to university."

When asked, "If you had your choice, what occupation would you like to follow as your life's work?", 25% chose professional careers and 42% selected white-collar work. This question was one of the few where there were really noticeable differences between males and females. While 39% of the male respondents selected professional careers as their choice, only 15% of the women did. On the other hand, 57% of the women opted for white-collar work and only 20% of the men did. Significantly, however, only 15% of the women (and 0% of the men) saw marriage as a "life's work."[29]

Many of these themes were picked up by other young people who agreed to take part in the intensive interviews. Although only 16 years old, the daughter of another railroad worker living in Edmonton seemed to have spent considerable time figuring out her options in life and reflecting on her experiences of schooling. She had completed Grade 11 in a local high school and was doing general office work in a hospital. She believed schools should be more flexible and more willing to offer advice to students. She suggested that the commercial high school offered too narrow a program but the regular high school was flawed, too, because it did not offer business courses. Fanny had taught herself to type in order to secure the job at the hospital and hoped one day to become an admitting officer. She suggested that trigonometry was not of much use to her in understanding sick people whereas psychology might have been but was not offered in the schools.

Like Marie, Fanny hoped to marry one day and was making plans for this by training herself to get along well with others and to be less moody and difficult. She was learning more about housekeeping and was reading books on agriculture in preparation for life on a farm. It was her view that there was more security to living on a farm because "you'll never starve." While Fanny anticipated getting married at about 25 and leaving the paid work force, she wanted her interim work to be interesting. For this reason, and because she acknowledged that she might never get married due to a shortage of men after the war, she wanted to work with people, not things.[30]

Neither Marie nor Fanny seemed unduly concerned about the possibility that they might not marry and were preparing themselves for the single life. For many young women like them, the experiences of the war may have suggested other options could realistically be considered. At the same time, many other young women continued to see marriage and child rearing either as their ultimate lot or goal in life, although they sensed that changes might be occurring and felt some unease about this. One young married mother living in Toronto commented, "... girls are faced with their most perplexing problems at the time of leaving school. You don't know what to do. You can't depend on getting married and you just wonder what's going to happen to you."[31] Similar fears about the future were expressed by a 23-year-old woman from Calgary when she was interviewed while working in an Ontario munitions plant. She noted that, "The girls know darn well they [i.e. factory owners] won't be taking them [women] back into industry after the war ... that's why they're buying bonds and saving every penny they can.... Some of the kids are good and scared." And so they should be said Amy because they had left school early to take work in the war industries. In her opinion, once the war was over they would find that their limited education would mean limited job options.[32]

While education played a large role in personal strategies for success, women, more often than men, expressed real regrets about lost opportunities for more education. Harriet, a 21-year-old woman in Woodstock, Ontario liked school but was forced to quit. Early in her interview she identifies family poverty as the reason she dropped out, but later she explains that her grandmother paid for her books and equipment while she was at school, her mother wanted her to finish high school but her father, a labourer, was physically abusive towards her and pressured her to abandon school. As she said, "he can't read or write himself and he figures he got along all right ... he used to say reading books would sure lead us astray."

Several other young women mention a father's "tyranny" as the reason they quit school and went out to work, often to marry soon after. One might conclude that they married to escape their fathers. This strategy could, of course, backfire as it did for the young woman from Woodstock. Prior to her marriage to a painter she had worked for more than two years in a knitting mill and for two months in a machine shop. Reflecting back on her choices she expressed regrets about quitting her machine shop job upon marriage. She liked the work because, "You could see what you were making and know that it was going to be of some use. I was making $45 a week doing piece work.... Gee, to think I gave it up for marriage."

Another young woman, along with all her sisters, consciously used marriage as a way to escape a violent father.

Although the father wanted his daughter to get as much education as possible, his behaviour forced her out of the home and into marriage with a union organizer at the age of 17. The circumstances are perhaps unique. The father, a barber, was a member of the Communist Party and objected when his daughter began to date a member of the CCF, especially when she adopted her boyfriend's politics. At one point the father locked his daughter in the house for three days to prevent her from attending a CCF rally. Finally, one night after returning from a CCF picnic, she found that her father had locked her out of the family home, she went to stay at her boyfriend's house and married him a month later.

Seven years after her marriage she still regretted her lack of a formal education but was determined that her two children would attend university and that her son would become a doctor or lawyer. She continued to work after marriage and at the time of the interview was a "trucker" in an industrial plant where she moved parts from one department to another. She would never be satisfied to stay at home she said, "That's the most monotonous thing in the world ... just taking care of two children and nothing else. Not for me. I'll always be active in one group or another." Indeed, this woman now saw her union, the United Auto Workers, as her "school."[33]

Most young people had ambivalent feelings about their education. On the one hand, most of them valued education per se and many expressed a real sadness about having to leave school for financial reasons. Comments throughout the intensive interviews are most telling. On having to leave school, one young woman said, "It almost broke my heart. I was dead set on becoming a nurse but there just wasn't any money for books and that was that." Another young woman wanted to attend the collegiate and complete her matric but was taken out of high school after one year because "... that's what Macedonians believe in for their girls — a little bit of school and then a lot of home training." At age 22 she longed for more education and said, "I still curse my father for not giving me a chance."

Young men in general talked less about being angry at having to leave school for financial reasons and do not seem as angry or hurt as the young women. Perhaps this is because they recognized that even without an education, their range of work options was wider than women's and that there were more opportunities for men to learn in the workplace and in public life. It is the young women who speak most often of going to evening classes, of teaching themselves to type or of engaging in other educational self-improvement activities. Indeed, education seems to be a life strategy more considered and used by the young women than by young men though both groups shared rather similar views on the strengths and weaknesses of the schooling they had received.

Surprisingly, perhaps, young people did not see job preparation as the most important purpose of schooling. When asked to rank a number of goals for secondary education, both young men and women placed "helping to think clearly on the problems of life" and "helping to understand modern society and the responsibilities of a citizen" above "getting a better job." Like Marie, they wanted school to provide "a real education," one which would help them make sense of the world round them. When asked to rate their schools in terms of how successful they had been in meeting those goals, young people were most disappointed in the school's failure to help them understand the complicated problems of modern life.[34] Similarly, as we have seen, young people faulted the schools for failing to prepare them for marriage and family life although women were somewhat more concerned about this than men (55% compared to 48%). Increasingly, young people wanted "thorough instruction in and discussion of sex, marriage and home relationships."[35]

Another part of the concern of young women was with the inadequacy of their courses in domestic science. Much of this criticism focused on courses which were "unrealistic." As one young, married woman put it, "They teach you stuff that's for a real up to date home ... you'd think we were all upper class the way they give us stuff for luncheons and tea parties ... nothing for a working man's home. In your own kitchen you just don't have a whole lot of utensils handy and you can't take all day to make a white sauce."[36] Another young woman observed that the courses were so elementary that you could learn the same material from your mother in half the time. "It seems silly," she said, "to spend six months learning how to hem a tea towel."[37]

If some young women were critical of the ability of their domestic science courses to prepare them for the transition from school to unpaid employment in the home, young men often were no less scornful of manual training or high school technical education classes as preparation for paid employment. David, a 15-year-old male who had dropped out of school at the age of 14 and after completing grade six, thought manual training "wasn't bad" but "you spend all your time making something dizzy like a tie rack...[. I]t would have been better if we had been taught machinery so if you quit school you would know how to make a living."[38] He found that the only school subjects that really helped him at work were reading, writing and spelling. This is in keeping with the findings of the survey conducted by the CYC's Committee on Education.

When young people who had left school were asked to identify those subjects which had been most valuable to them since leaving school, a large majority opted for English (or French where that was the first language) and mathematics. These findings match the findings of a 1950 study of young people who had left school two years earlier. In this study boys ranked mathematics first and English second while shop courses came in a distant third. Girls selected English as the most important subject while commercial courses and mathematics ran neck-and-neck for second and third place.[39] Given what we know about the growing importance of clerical and office work for young women in the twentieth century, this is probably not surprising.

There is something particularly significant about the high ranking given to English and mathematics because young workers indicated "that these are the subjects which have been of most value to them not only in their jobs but in all their activities."[40] While young people wanted schooling to offer some preparation for work in terms of a good basic grounding in the traditional academic subjects, they rarely saw this preparation in terms of training in narrowly defined or job-specific work skills.

Young people actually used part-time work as a way to

acquaint themselves with the specific demands of the workplace. Jennie talked about her Christmas job at the Post Office which was "not so hot." But, she said, a variety of part-time jobs are good for young people: "It helps them to understand how it feels to be working in different kinds of ways. I mean if you have a monotonous tiring job like at the Post Office then you know what some people have to put up with in their dull little jobs."[41] An experience of the workplace taught 17-year-old Donald something too. "I want to go back to school more than ever after seeing the men at Canada Packers day after day, year after year, picking [plucking?] chickens. You can get a lot with money that you can't have otherwise."[42] Young people also felt that it was part-time jobs that taught them how to work and gave them self-confidence.[43]

With respect to employment, young people wanted two things. From the Canadian government they wanted action to ensure a full employment policy and social security. From the schools they wanted supportive and informed vocational guidance and a solid grounding in the traditional three R's which the young viewed as "a practical education." In addition, they wanted the schools to provide them with an education that would help them understand social problems, think clearly about political and economic issues and prepare them for marriage and family life. For young Canadians in the 1940s, their interest was in more than the transition from school to paid employment. They wanted the schools to make provision for the over-all transition to adult life. A brief from a labour youth organization puts this position exactly. "There is too much emphasis on job training and too little on cultural education. Schools are actually subsidizing industry.... The whole cultural field should be opened up in literature, science, to prepare our minds ... to go out and investigate questions that we meet in life."[44]

NOTES:
1. Examples of these debates in the period prior to 1950 can be found in G. Kealey, ed., *Canada Investigates Industrialism: The Royal Commission on the Relations of Labour and Capital, 1889*, reprinted and abridged. Toronto: University of Toronto Press, 1973; Government of Canada, *Royal Commis-*

sion on Industrial Training and Technical Education: Report of the Commissioners. Ottawa: King's Printer, 1913; Government of Canada, *Final Report of the National Employment Commission*. Ottawa: King's Printer, 1938; Government of Canada, *Final Report of the Advisory Committee on Reconstruction*. Ottawa: King's Printer, 1944. For an interesting discussion of the historical roots of public policies in the U.S. which both blame and seek salvation in educational solutions for economic ills, see Barbara Finkelstein, "Dollars and Dreams: Classrooms as Fictitious Message Systems, 1790–1930," *History of Education Quarterly*, vol. 31, no. 4 (Winter, 1991), pp. 463–487.

2. A recent example of a national survey of youth is found in Donald Posterski and Reginald Bibby, *Canada's Youth "Ready for Today": A Comprehensive Survey of 15-24 Year Olds*. Ottawa: The Canadian Youth Foundation, 1988.

3. One discussion of the work of the CYC can be found in Linda M. Ambrose, "'Working Day and Night Helping Dick': Women in Post-War Planning on the Canadian Youth Commission, 1942–48," *Historical Studies in Education/Revue d'histoire de l'education*, 3:1 (Spring, 1991), pp. 75–92.

4. Rebecca Priegert Coulter, "Managing Youth Unemployment: The Dominion-Provincial Youth Training Programme, 1937–40," *Journal of Educational Administration and Foundations* (in press, 1993).

5. See, for example, H. A. Weir, "Unemployed Youth," in L. Richter, ed., *Canada's Unemployment Problem*. Toronto: Macmillan, 1939, pp. 111–171; Kenneth Woodsworth, *Canadian Youth Comes of Age*. Toronto: Ryerson Press, 1939; National Archives of Canada (hereafter NAC), Records of the Royal Commission on Dominion-Provincial Relations, RG 33/23, vol. 12, exhibit 335, "Youth's Eye View of Some Problems Concerned with Getting Married" by Ontario Young Men's Council of the YMCA, n.d. 1935?, and vol. 13, exhibit 336, "Youth in the Next Decade: Reports of the Committee of Twelve" by St. John, New Brunswick YMCA Project, 1935; Alistair M. Stewart, *The Youth Problem of Manitoba*. Winnipeg: Manitoba Economic Survey Board, 1939.

6. A good example of this kind of discussion can be found in Government of Alberta, Department of Education, *Annual Report*, 1938, p. 9.

7. NAC, Canadian Welfare Council Papers, MG 28, I 10, vol. 83, file 594, Canadian Welfare Council Survey on Youth Employment, 1941; vol. 77, file 564, Child Welfare-Child Labour Laws, 1943.

8. On the work of Margaret Davis, see Ambrose, "'Working Day and Night Helping Dick'...."

9. See, for example, the structure of the Committee on Education which was chaired by G. Fred McNally, Alberta's Deputy Minister of Education and Commission member. The committee membership is described in Canadian Youth Commission, *Youth Challenges the Educators*. Toronto: Ryerson Press, 1946, p. iv.

10. Canadian Youth Commission, *Youth and Jobs in Canada*. Toronto: Ryerson Press, 1945; CYC, *Youth Challenges the Educators*.

11. NAC, Canadian Youth Commission Papers, MG 28, I 11, vol. 52, file "Youth Commission Survey, June 1944."

12. This survey and the results can be found in CYC, *Youth Challenges the Educators*.

13. NAC, Canadian Youth Commission Papers, MG 28, I 11, vols. 45–52, "Intensive Interviews."

14. CYC, *Youth and Jobs*, p. 1.

15. NAC, CYC Papers, MG 28, I 11, vol. 28, file 1(2e), Calgary Conference Composite Brief, 27 May, 1944.

16. NAC, CYC Papers, MG 28, I 11, vol. 62, file 12 (5a), "Report of the Winnipeg Youth Conference...Youth Also Plan," 28–30 April, 1944.

17. Two key works are Neil Sutherland, *Children in English-Canadian Society: Framing the Twentieth-Century Consensus*. Toronto: University of Toronto Press, 1976 and Patricia T. Rooke and R.L. Schnell, *Discarding the Asylum: From Child Rescue to the Welfare State in Canada (1800-1950)*. Latham, MD: University Press of America, 1983.

18. NAC, CYC Papers, MG 28, I 11, vol. 28, file 1 (2e); CYC, *Youth Challenges the Educators*, p. iv.

19. NAC, CYC Papers, MG 28, I 11, vol. 7, file 59 (g), Tuttle to Ready, 15 March, 1945.

20. Since Protestants usually controlled local committees, this was an unusual circumstance and one which would later lead to considerable sectarian acrimony among the adults. NAC, CYC Papers, MG 28, I 11, vol. 28, file 1 (2e).

21. *Ibid.*

22. NAC, CYC Papers, MG 28, I 11, vol. 28, file 1 (2e), Cooper to Hugg, 22 February 1944. The Canadian Youth Congress is discussed briefly in Paul Axelrod, "The Student Movement of the 1930s," in Paul Axelrod and John G. Reid, eds., *Youth, University and Canadian Society: Essays in the Social History of Higher Education*. Kingston, Montreal and London: McGill-Queen's University Press, 1989, pp. 216–246.

23. "Canadian Youth," *Ponoka Herald*, 20 July, 1944.

24. NAC, CYC Papers, MG 28, I 11, vol. 7, file 59 (g), Ready to Davis, 27 March, 1944.

25. NAC, CYC Papers, MG 28, I 11, vol. 26, file 7 (i) 2d.

26. *Ibid.*

27. "Permanent Youth Organization...," *Edmonton Bulletin*, 13 November, 1944.

28. This interview is found in NAC, CYC Papers, MG 28, I 11, vol. 45,

series (c) 9, Youth Survey, Intensive Interviews. These are closed files which I had permission to access provided the identities of the informants were protected. Consequently, all the names of the interviewees are pseudonyms.

29. NAC, CYC Papers, MG 28, I 11, vol. 52, unfiled.

30. NAC, CYC Papers, MG 28, I 11, vol. 49, "Intensive Interviews-Alberta."

31. NAC, CYC Papers, MG 28, I 11, vol. 47, series (c)9, "Intensive Interviews-Ontario."

32. NAC, CYC Papers, MG 28, I 11, vol. 49, file "Intensive Interviews-Alberta."

33. *Ibid.*

34. CYC, *Youth Challenges the Educators*, pp. 3–12.

35. NAC, CYC Papers, MG 28, I 11, vol. 33, file 11 (3c), Summary of the findings of David Edgar Mahood, "A Study of the Opinions and Attitudes of Grade XII Students Concerning Three Aspects of their High School Education: Namely Extra-Curricular Activities, Curricular Content and Method, and Behaviour Guidance," M.Ed. thesis, University of Saskatchewan, 1944.

36. NAC, CYC Papers, MG 28, I 11, vol. 48, series (c)9, "Intensive Interviews-Ontario."

37. *Ibid.*

38. NAC, CYC Papers, MG 28, I 11, vol. 46, series (c)9, Intensive Interviews-Ontario" (male), pt. 1.

39. The Canadian Research Committee on Practical Education, *Two Years After School*. Toronto: Canadian Research Committee on Practical Education, 1951, pp. 17, 55.

40. *Ibid.*, p. 17.

41. NAC, CYC Papers, MG 28, I 11, vol. 48, series (c)9, "Intensive Interviews-Ontario" (female), pt. 3.

42. NAC, CYC Papers, MG 28, I 11, vol. 46, series (c)9, "Intensive Interviews-Ontario" (male), pt. 1.

43. *Two Years After School*, p. 64.

44. Quoted in CYC, *Youth Challenges Educators*.

Chapter Five

Labour Education
Working Knowledge At The Core Of Learning

Jeffry Piker

> *North American culture— high and low, popular or elitist —presents almost nowhere the realities of daily work.*
> (Tom Wayman, editor, *Paperwork: Contemporary Poems from the Job*, 1991, "Introduction", p. xv.)

In a society that so successfully avoids serious consideration of what work is like, while at the same time so regularly devalues workers, it is hardly surprising that we accomplish the transition from school to work so poorly for working people. As British Columbia poet and anthologist of workers' poetry, Tom Wayman, has pointed out:

> What happens to human beings on the job is not considered a topic for major consideration by our school curriculums, even though working is the activity that eventually will occupy most of the working lives of every student (Wayman, 1991, p. xvi).

When work does somehow find its way into aspects of schooling, the form it usually takes excludes workers themselves from the process and content of what is being taught (and learned). Elsewhere in this volume, Nancy Jackson describes how our schools present work-related knowledge and skills as "external," "naturally occurring" phenomena, which apparently exist merely as "performances" from which "knowing subjects" can then be effectively removed. Skills become more real than workers (in the same way that productivity is more important than work).

Even the way educators take for granted the importance of the concept, 'skill' — rather than stress its much more personal cousin, 'technique' — contributes to the externalization (of work) and objectification (of workers) in the teaching/learning process. 'Skill' is an outsider's term; 'technique' is an insider's term. It is the outsider's view that dominates Canadian education for work:

> Technique is ... a more useful term (than skill) because it indicates a form of interaction with tools, environment, and other workers that connotes expertise and esoteric knowledge.... Technique is the 'shaping principle' of an occupation.... Within the occupation it is known as 'knowing the trade', or being a 'good mechanic' or a 'good hand'. Outside of the work group it is generally referred to as 'skill'... (McCarl, 1976, p. 7).

What would education for work be like if it started from a position of genuine respect for working knowledge and for the interests and concerns of the working people that possess it? How would its process and content differ from the curricula our schools currently lump under the heading 'transition from school to work'?

A useful place to begin to look for answers to this question is in the field of labour education. All across Canada labour unions run courses for their own members. Lasting from a few days to a few weeks, these courses address a wide array of topics. Some focus on the specific 'tools' of union activity, while others take up complex issues of more general concern to the labour movement. Labour education course titles include, for example: Health and Safety, Women in the Labour Movement, Collective Bargaining, Labour History, Pensions, Employment Equity, Tech. Change, Shop Steward, Workers' Compensation, Labour Law and Adjustment Planning.

Within the hallowed halls of the education profession, labour education is seldom acknowledged as a substantial and important undertaking. Simply based on its scope, however — not to mention, its important outcomes! — this is a serious and unfortunate oversight. Jim Turk, education director of the Ontario Federation of Labour, has observed that more than 100,000 Canadian workers enrol in labour education courses each year. (cited in Procenko, 1991.) In a background conversation for this article, Danny Mallett, the CLC's National Coordinator for Educational Services, recently estimated that there are 13–14,000 labour educators currently active across Canada — 4–5,000 in Ontario alone. Most of these people are themselves full-time workers in jobs and sectors directly relevant to the content of the courses they teach. They are often called 'worker-trainers.'

Unionists themselves commonly refer to labour education courses as 'schools' — an interesting and perhaps ironic use of the word, given the memories many working people carry of the ways in which, and the extent to which, they had been excluded from their own formal schooling. Gord Wilson, president of the OFL:

> On reflection, looking back upon my educational experiences, I was far more compromised in school than I ever have been by any manager or government official. My formal education experience was not very pleasant, and I think my experience has been shared by many others (1989).

It is as though they have finally discovered, in labour education, an educational format where they feel respected as learners, and where the organization of teaching and learning treats their own experiences, questions, concerns, knowledge and competences as resources rather than handicaps, located at the centre of the education rather than off to the side. That they still want to use the term 'school' reflects an optimism that is refreshing, to say the least.

The Labour Education Alternative

What is it about labour education that counteracts the 'exclusionary,' 'objectivized' and 'externalized' nature of traditional education for work? This is a large and many-sided question.

Its answer would involve a much more substantial investigation than what is possible here. (Such inquiry would be well worth the effort — both for the values mainline educators could derive for their own work, and for the insights labour educators could gain for theirs.)

As a starting point, five essential characteristics of labour education seem generally important for its substance and effectiveness. Each differs from what is commonly the case in traditional education for work.

1. Workers are present *as workers*. Their own personal productivity — as makers of things or deliverers of services — is given prominence and respect. They view their fellow learners as fellow workers: 'in solidarity'. Pride is therefore present, for themselves and for each other.

2. *Working knowledge* is itself the basis of teaching and learning. Students are there to learn how to be more effective union members at their workplaces. Relevance is in the foreground. In Jackson's terms, "... the worker (is put) at the centre of the action ...(,) the learner (is presumed to have) dignity and power" (1992, p. 16). A praxis of action and reflection is readily available.

3. The traditional teacher/learner *hierarchy is restructured*. It is flattened considerably — although not entirely removed, since the 'teacher' ('trainer,' 'facilitator,' etc.) role is still present. Because the worker/trainer is partly a worker like all the trainees, possibilities for empathy and mutuality are greatly increased. This has profound effects on the structure and quality of communication within the classroom — in both directions.

4. Labour education takes for granted the *analytic skills of workers*. Rather than view working people as inevitably non-theoretical (with a learning style a high-school tech. teacher once described to me as 'monkey see, monkey do'), these courses consciously and intentionally integrate both general principles and specific applications within course curriculum. And the learners, for their part, bring both the specific and the general from their own backgrounds the

'manual' and the 'mental' — problems and accomplishments rooted in first-hand experience, and insights and interpretations based on that experience. Analysis (what some would, and others would not, want to call 'theory') is neither treated nor regarded as something alien or unpleasant.
5. Aspects of the *political context* of course content ('subject matter') are made explicit. Particular relationships of power become key components of curriculum, depending on the content focus of each course; for example: the labour/management context, the nature of supervision and decision-making, the role of laws and government, union structure, the dynamics of capitalism, the organization of communities, the operations of bureaucracy. Because the politics of course content are explicitly addressed, the politics of teaching/learning process can be given serious consideration as well.

The labour education framework generates practices which give it a particular shape and character. For example, course titles specify aspects of work or work context, rather than names of disciplines generated in non-work (mainly academic) settings. Training manuals guide and inform course agendas. Resource handouts are frequent. Seating is in the round or in small groups. Videos, overheads and flipcharts are preferred kinds of equipment. The overall tone is more like a workshop than a traditional classroom. Learners are called 'participants' or 'trainees,' rather than 'students.'

Testing, in any explicit and formal sense, is seldom done. Attendance is required, but what is stressed is active participation and involvement in learning. The only 'mark' that is given is an informal kind of 'credit' for having completed the course. This credit is nowhere registered, nor can it be exchanged for certification in institutional circles. Still, course graduates themselves know and remember which courses they have taken, and can gain support and encouragement for their education from within their local unions and bargaining units.

Discussion (both plenary and small-group) is a key method for teaching and learning in labour education. Participation in discussion takes a variety of forms: asking questions or stating problems (not always the same thing), answering questions or suggesting solutions, providing resource information, figuring out case studies, describing personal experiences, stating agreements and disagreements, or making analytic interpretations.

Through discussion, the first-hand experiences of students become, collectively, a major 'textbook' for the course. They serve as examples of general points. In combination, they produce analytic interpretations. When put as questions or problems, they focus course inquiry. A significant challenge for the worker/trainer role is to integrate discussion into the content and structure of the course agenda. Discussion takes time, resists tidiness of focus, and often proceeds in unpredictable directions. On the other hand, discussion helps to sustain energy and enthusiasm for learning, and grounds more difficult concepts and information within personal frameworks.

Worker/trainers usually have little formal training as teachers. Often, however, they have been trainees themselves, and have probably also attended train-the-trainer workshops. And all of them have undergone years of traditional schooling. There is an inevitable dialectic between what they remember (and do not necessarily appreciate) school as having been like for themselves in the past, and what they want labour education to be like for participants in the present.

Because trainers and trainees share so many background experiences, possibilities for empathy (in both directions) are abundant. Learner support for teaching and teacher support for learning are strong. The notion of 'expertise,' existing above and beyond the learners' world is greatly demystified. If worker/trainers have learned it, trainees (who are also workers) can be readily expected, and can expect themselves, to learn it too.

Learners And teachers

Labour education can provide powerful and very useful resources for the reconstruction of the relationship between school and work. This is not, certainly, because the field of labour education has refined all the problems out of its method and content. Far from it. Like any complicated and ambitious educational endeavour, this field is still struggling with its own problems, shortcomings, contradictions and inadequate resources.

There is often too strong a tendency, for example, to treat

training manuals like recipe books, with a corresponding undervaluing of trainer skills (and trainer skill development). Disinclination to evaluate participant learning leaves labour education courses with at best sporadic and anecdotal impressions of learner outcomes. It also provides a weak basis for ongoing program evaluation.

Indeed, calling labour education a 'field' may be something of an over-statement — even within the labour movement, much less outside it. Labour educators are not, apparently, in substantial, effective and ongoing communication with each other across unions — regarding such vital and shared issues as course and program objectives, pedagogical methods and instructional resources, train-the-trainer techniques, learner and program evaluation, and program development strategies. Some unions are more willing and able than others to invest time and money in educational programs. None can generate as much money for member education as they need or want.

However, the point to stress is that, despite its problems and struggles, labour education has produced for itself a form of teaching and learning which locates learners' competences, knowledge, experiences and potential for concrete action at the centre of the process. It has discarded the 'mental/manual' (or 'heads' and 'hands') distinction that traditionally devalued the worth and complexity of the working knowledge of working people. It has identified the importance of empathy as an instructional 'skill,' and it has capitalized on the value of discussion as a vehicle for learning. It has restructured the traditional hierarchy that places teachers so far above learners, and curriculum content so far outside the realities of learners' everyday lives. As an experienced labour educator recently pointed out, "You can't get up there feeling holier than thou. These people know me, I work with them. I can't pretend to be 'the expert.'"

Educators in traditional school settings would benefit from careful consideration of the structure and pedagogy of labour education. By the same token, labour educators could improve their own courses and practices through increased contact with the working knowledge of professional educators.

Unfortunately, other than in a select few, shared forums (such as *Our Schools/Our Selves*), where progressive educators of many stripes can shed the burdens and blinkers of habit and inclination, it is difficult to foresee how and where this kind of useful dialogue is going to come about. Professional educators too often seem to carry a least a disregard, and too often a kind of disdain, for the seriousness and significance of union-based education. And for their part, labour educators have perhaps not yet developed enough stability and security in their role to allow them to move beyond their critique of formal schooling to tap the wealth of educational skills, techniques and insights that many teachers really do possess.

The objectification and externalization of working knowledge that has characterized schooling for work in Canadian society has apparently spun off a host of related contradictions that will make genuinely progressive reform of educational institutions even more difficult to accomplish. The deceptions, myths and half-truths that our children learn as students linger with them and sometimes come back into play, even when those same students later become teachers themselves, and want to undo some of the damage that they know, first-hand, has been done.

Jeffry Piker is an educational consultant and writer who lives in Kingston, Ontario.

References

Nancy S. Jackson, "Rethinking Vocational Knowledge", working draft, Feb., 1992.

Robert S. McCarl, Jr., "Occupational Folklife: A Theoretical Hypothesis," in R. Byington, ed., *Working Americans: Contemporary Approaches to Occupational Folklife*, Smithsonian Folklife Studies, Vol. 3, 1978, pp. 3–18.

Sonya Procenko, "Class Conscious: Labour Studies Programs," *Our Times*, May, 1991, pp. 17–19.

Tom Wayman, ed., *Paperwork — Contemporary Poems from the Job*. Madiera Park, B.C.: Harbour Publishing, 1991.

Gord Wilson, "Getting an Education the Hard Way," *It's Our Own Knowledge: Labour, Public Education and Skills Training*. Toronto: Our Schools/Our Selves, Nov., 1989, pp. 9–18.

Chapter Six

Dropped Stitches
The Absence Of Domestic Labour In Discussions Of Schooling And Work

Madeleine R. Grumet
*Brooklyn College,
City University of New York*

For centuries schooling interrupted work, and was wedged into the winters when the fields lay fallow. Even after industrialization, the relationship between school and work cannot be seen as literal or linear. The credential that schooling supplies more often functions to signify class position and cultural capital than it does to provide preparation for the tasks and competencies that particular jobs require. Nevertheless, as governments attempt to rationalize weak economies, unfavourable trade balances and products that are no longer competitive on world markets, the relationship between school and work is portrayed as causal, bonded in an equation of blame. The onus of failure is shifted from management to workers, from workers to schools, from schools to teachers, from teachers to children and their families. The trajectory of this relentless referral moves from the top of the hierarchy to the bottom. It is assumed that the organization at the top of the pyramid is both necessary and sufficient and that the economy suffers from the failure of those below to meet the standards and supply the energy and commitment that industry requires.

In this essay I will argue that reproduction and production are wound into one, integrated system and that any theory of work that addresses the relations of workers to each other must start from an analysis of the workplace of reproduction and the domestic relations that are sedimented in the biography of anyone who works for a living.

Recognizing Domestic Labour

Implicit in the phrase "the transition from school to work," that serves as the focus for our deliberations is the assumption that these two institutions, schooling and wage labour, constitute the major, if not only, domains in the geography and biography of human labour. Domestic labour, its politics, rewards and relations to the material world, remains invisible, a backstage area, (Epstein, 193), and I am reminded of the literal meaning of the word *obscene*: behind the scene. Cynthia Fuchs Epstein suggests that information about the family is often invisible to even its own members, and that the segregation of its male and female members, often produces discrepant data (193). Men, she claims, tend to under-report their domestic work and to belittle their wives' public work, an investment which the wives, themselves, often underplay (1988, 208). It is amusing to see the metaphor of "discrepant data" used to euphemize the contradictions, tensions and shifts, betrayals and repudiations that emerge in narrative accounts of family life.

In *Bitter Milk: Women and Teaching* I have argued that the elision of home in talk about schooling is no accident. The 'dropped stitches' of this title is also a euphemism — entire rows have been ripped out. In industrialized cultures schooling functions to transfer children from women to men, moving them from the so called 'private' domain to public space, from their intimate and personal identities — embodied, dancing to the rhythms and sounds of home — to their social identities represented in nominal, rational and systematic identifications that sustain association with the labour and class position of their fathers.[1]

Schools are not the only institutions that train us to turn our gaze away from home. The feminization of domesticity can make home hard to find, even in our mother's houses. When scenes of the kitchen or the bathroom appear in magazines, on billboards and television screens, they promote the female regulation of the body, through grooming and style, through cleaning, clothing, and commodified addiction.[2] So bathrooms are deodorised, toilet bowls are scrubbed, clothing is decontaminated from its contact with the leaking body. Food is wrapped, and packaged, served and put away. The sauce in the bottle is, we are told, as good as mama's, but it takes no time to prepare and leaves no sticky mess on the stove.

I am not suggesting that home is a closed environment, or that the culture of the family does not take up the ideologies of the larger culture as it budgets resources, selects a dining set for the kitchen or decides who will dry the dishes or return the soda bottles to the supermarket. Nevertheless, the study of domestic labour and family culture cannot be collapsed into public images of family life. In "Curriculum and the Art of Daily Life," I argue that domestic culture is not just adsorbed, but that it is actively constructed, through labour and through the constant interpretation, application and transformation of cultural norms (Grumet, 1991). Because as children, we are its recipients, we tend to think of it as given, rather than constructed, and even when our contact with different households reveals the great multitude of ways that people organize themselves to share time and space and love, we tend to collapse our perceptions into generalizations about their character or culture, oblivious to the improvizations embedded in what appear to be the most traditional rituals.[3]

I have yet to see a television commercial where someone opens the refrigerator and drinks orange juice or milk straight from the carton. But I can tell you that if my children had been so disciplined, they would have expired long ago from thirst. The worst offender was, of course, my son, who suffered the indignation of his sisters as soon as they were old enough to take charge of regulating their own and other's domestic bodies. And when, on those rare occasions, I raised that soggy spout to my own mouth to gulp down the cold milk, unimpeded by pitcher, mug or cup, I made sure that I was not observed.

I indulge this piece of domestic confession (there are plenty of others where that came from), because I want to make it clear that this paper is not about what people really do in those places we call home. This paper is about what people say they do. More importantly, it is about what people don't say. Domestic experience is silenced because it contradicts the ideology of maternal sacrifice and regulation, because the boundaries between people that domesticity is expected to construct and fortify erode and crumble and are, over time, continually renegotiated and redesigned. Domestic experience is silenced because, despite our commercials and courtesies, it violates the mores, methods and mechanisms of the workplace.

Helena Michie traces the muting and metamorphosis of domesticity in the post-industrialization novels of the Victorian era. In *The Flesh Made Word*, Michie notes the absence of domestic labour from representation in Victorian novels. Women's work and hunger are kept from depiction because, she argues, they are associated with a woman's body, hence her sexuality. Michie attributes her interest in this inquiry to her own adolescent fascination with Dorothea, the heroine of Middlemarch, reminding me of my own adolescent fascination with *Jane Eyre, Tess of the D'Urbervilles, A Rose in Bloom* and *Pride and Prejudice*; all sagas of the struggles of bright and passionate young women to deny their energy and sexuality.

The anxieties and frailties of the Victorian heroine are custom tailored to her inhibition and renunciation of enterprise. Leisure-class heroines, no longer taken up with the tasks of subsistence economy, relinquish robust activity, sensuous appearance and hearty appetite to working-class women. Should the lady stumble into hard times and wage labour, she does not assume the vigor of her working-class sisters but like Sister Carrie, she falls vulnerable to disease, and to moral and physical degradation. Michie's analysis offers us a glimpse of the way that a woman's body serves as a metaphor for the positions of women and their labouring husbands in the sexual, familial, and economic politics of newly industrialized England. As production leaves the homestead to move to urban factories and offices, the sensuousness of family life is transformed into domesticity: industrialization's refuge, denial and status symbol. And I feel these Victorian compunctions constricting academic discourse as we gather to discuss the transition from school to work in post-industrial North America, 1992.

If Michie suggests that domestic labour is banished from the Victorian text in the process of establishing class and gender conventions for industrial capitalism, Third-World capitalism also hides domestic labour, exploiting domestic skill as native talent. The assumption that what women do "comes naturally" makes domestic labour invisible. Elson and Pearson refer to this naturalization of female labour in citing Sharpston's study of the factory work of Moroccan girls (1991). Taught the assembly under magnification of memory planes for computers, these accomplished young women are still perceived as 'unskilled' or 'semi-skilled.' Their competence is attributed to nimble fingers and manual dexterity, ignoring the skills they have developed learning to sew in their own homes. Marxist theory encodes and legitimizes this denigration by defining domestic labour under capitalism as producing use-values rather than exchange values. Harris explains: "Where commodity relations prevail, the circulation of use-values as use-values is effectively curtailed. Conversely where commodity exchange is absent, use-values are produced and consumed within an integrated circuit; this latter economic form is significantly termed in classical Marxism the 'natural economy'" (1991, 142).

Conflations of female gender with domestic labour, repression of domestic labour, of hunger and sexuality are echoed in the autobiographical narratives written by women who have been my students in universities in the U.S. and Canada. For the last 20 years as I have taught in different colleges and universities, I have asked students to write three short narratives of educational experience, inviting them to write any story that they associate with that phrase. They are encouraged to locate that story in any setting — it needn't be school — and to present all the physical detail they can remember/imagine associated with the event they recount.

Stories often describe travel to foreign places, deaths of loved ones, parents, grandparents, siblings and pets, car accidents, physical injury, first school experiences, defiance of unfair teachers. When the stories recount work, the exhaustion of housepainting or struggles with sadistic managers, that work rarely takes place in the home. When domestic labour has appeared, it is involved with assuming the tasks of an invalid or dying mother:

> One day, I think it was June twenty-ninth, 1975, I was told by my mother that she had cancer. She wasn't going to die, but she would have to have her left breast removed. My first reaction was one of shock, and then relief because she would be cured by the surgery.
>
> When mom went into the hospital I had the burden of running the household. Dad works all day, and my brothers (I have two) are no big help. I did the laundry, cleaned the house and did all the cooking. It was summer vacation so there was no school. My mother was in the hospital for ten days.
>
> The responsibility of taking care of a family was an educational experience in itself. I had to learn how to separate dark socks from white underwear, and to remember to put the garbage out on Tuesdays.
>
> My mother had a semi-radical breast operation and there was only about a 10% chance that she would ever have this type of cancer again. A fact that worried me was something I had read in a pamphlet. It said that daughters of breast cancer victims are 3 times as likely to get breast cancer than normal women. I then found out that this was only a theory, since the actual causes of breast cancer have yet to be discovered. Learning about cancer was very educational. Cancer wasn't a subject discussed that much in our family until my mother found out she had it.
>
> The day my mother came home we had a surprise party for it was her fortieth birthday. She is so unbelievable in the way she handled her illness. My father was very supportive, and I think that helped her a great deal. Our family became even closer after this and we talk about cancer more freely now.

The educational experience in schools does not allow for the learning of responsibility. A person has to learn responsibility at home. I learned what being responsible meant through my mother's tragedy. I think I would have eventually learned responsibility even if my mother had never had cancer, but it certainly wouldn't of happened that summer.

Against the background of Michie's readings it is not surprising to see housework connected to a mother's body, to a cancer that threatens to break the boundaries that contain health and life. As this daughter assumes her mother's labour, she fears her identification with her mother's body. She interrupts the song of intimacy, of love for and identification with her mother with the presence of her father, and generalizes the intimacy that she has feared and celebrated to the family. Here the pun on responsibility is salient. Schools cannot teach responsibility because the persons to whom we have the strongest responses are in our families and not in our schools. Furthermore, responsibility is not only an obligation it is a privilege. When the regulation and order of the home is contained within the knowledge and labour of one person, the mother, the agency of other people in that household is diminished. If the home, its walls and floors, its goods and treasures, constitutes the only material reality that a woman can shape and celebrate as a consequence of her labour, it collapses into her thing, a memento to the relations it once contained.

Even when domestic labour is shared, it may still belong to Mom. Here is another narrative where female competence is, at first, naturalized and then repudiated, but not without guilt:

> We are seven members within my household this is, including my parents. I am the second oldest and the oldest of the girls. Since I am the oldest of the girls I was expected to help with the house chores. My sister also helped out once in a while. I often arrived home from school later than I was expected. That was not a problem as long as I did what I was supposed to do. That was to complete my homework, study, and let me not forget my duty at home.
>
> My sister and I did the dishes every night after dinner. We took turns. We each had a week. I washed dishes every other week. I didn't enjoy this, but I also didn't seem to mind either. Some-

times I wanted to hurry, especially when I wanted to watch T.V. I would set the dishes in order quickly. First the larger plates then the smaller bowls, later all the glasses and cups and the last were the knives, forks and spoons. Usually after dinner my mother would make coffee which I hated because this was only more dishes for me to do. She sometimes would take out these off-white very small delicate coffee cups my aunt had once gave her for Christmas. Everyone liked them. They had an oriental style and were trimmed with a gold colour making them look very expensive.

One night she took out her coffee set, poured some coffee for her and my father, and again it was my week for the dishes. When they finished, I very quickly cleared the table and one of them just slipped from my hand. From the living room my mother heard it fall and break. Every time I look at the other three coffee cups, I could still hear my mother yelling from the other room "that it had better not been the coffee cups your aunt gave me." From that day on I hated those cups and I still do. Every time my mom wants to use them she always brings it up and she always says how she was unable to replace them because they were so difficult to find.

I am twenty-one years old now, this was about nine years ago and I still hate those cups.

In this narrative, where mother is alive and well, domestic labour is referred from her to her daughters, naturally endowed by their sex for the drying of dishes. The opportunity to order this domestic world is celebrated as the daughter displays her method. First the larger plates, then the smaller bowls, glasses, cups, then knives, forks and spoons. I must admit that I still get some pleasure from determining where what will be placed in the dishwasher. I try not to show my discomfort when a someone else in the family improvises on my scheme, having chosen long ago to relinquish control in order to do something other than dishes. Still, I wince when I find the bowls where I usually place the plates, or when the mugs are wedged into the channel I reserve for the glasses.

In this narrative maternal authority is resented and the fetish of female domesticity is contained in the fragile, expensive, exotic coffee service. The daughter suggests that the cups merely look expensive, suggesting that their status is as fragile as their composition. The cups belong to women, passing from aunt, to mother, to daughter, even though they hold a father's coffee. They provide the ritual of intimacy of husband and wife that excludes the daughter just as the ritual of dish drying excludes her sister, isolating this daughter in labour that she can imitate but not own.

Again these are written accounts. They are narratives of female experience and even though their writers wear blue jeans and cowboy boots, I still hear the skirts of Jane and Tess and Emma rustling among the coffee cups, the dark socks and the garbage pails. Sociologists might not be content with these accounts. Perhaps they are merely echoes of the genre and personae of the Victorian novels present in the high school literary curriculum and extended, with modifications, into soap operas, where hunger and labour are still taboo but sexuality flourishes. While these stories may not be accurate representations of these writers domestic labour, they were the ones they chose to tell. They encode the way the writers see themselves within the labour community of their family, they suggest the perimeters of their enterprise, the politics of activity within their homes, and the pleasure of being the one who orders that world. I remember the leitmotif that Virginia Woolf creates for Mrs. Ramsey, the matriarch of *To the Lighthouse*, "she would open windows, she would shut doors."

Both of these writers were enrolled in courses leading to teacher certification. I want to suggest that the identifications and rebellions that they record as part of their domestic work are processes of affiliation and differentiation that they will carry into their activity as students and as teachers. I am not suggesting that these narratives provide a template that will stamp their later enterprise with a pattern to be endlessly repeated. Rather, I suggest that as we shift locations, from home to school, to work we use this migration as occasions to alter our practice, to re-position ourselves in the new setting, where the losses of the past may be redeemed.

I wonder what the breaker of cups will think about the canon, about those texts and classics arranged to look expensive, knowledge that belongs to someone else, that resists her own order and vision. I wonder what the mother's helper in the first narrative will expect of the men who share her workplace. Will she excuse them from duty, pleased to characterize them in ways that justify their absence, confusing her rejection of them with their passivity or refusal. Will she hide her identification with the women she works with in subordination to male bureaucracies in homophobic flight from the power as well as the vulnerability of women? Who will sort the laundry in her classroom? Who will plan the meals? Who will take out the garbage?

Rarely does domestic labour find its way into these narratives of educational experience. That is not because the hundreds of other student writers, male as well female, did not experience domestic labour. Surely they made beds, cared for siblings, started cooking fires or spilled nail polish on the couch. Perhaps they do not think of the feeding, sheltering and sustaining of families as educational. Perhaps, well trained to understand that schooling is about the repudiation of home, they would not write domestic labour within the context of a college course just as they would not write about their appetites, or their eating disorders, or their sexuality.

Many will find this reticence appropriate, admire its discretion and resist the effort to bridge the gap that separates private from public experience with autobiographical narratives. Nevertheless, when the knowledge and experience generated at home is not brought to language, it fails to function as knowledge. In order to achieve the functional status of knowledge, experience must be symbolized in a code that invites reflection, comparison and revision. When domestic experience is buried below speech, it is not available to the person who needs to understand it in order to understand the relations in school and in the workplace that exist in relation to it. Practical knowledge is not knowledge at all until it can be symbolized and stored so that it provides a frame for the analysis of later experience.

This stillness mutes the hum, the banging doors, falling cups, the taking turns, the ducking out, the pride, celebration and the bitter resentment of domestic work. Home is the first place of both labour and consciousness. But like our student writers, rarely do we acknowledge its precedence. We take the middle stop on this route to wage labour — school — and present it as an origin. In that displacement we repeat the presumption of patriarchy that compensates for the inferential nature of paternity by claiming to be the cause.

In *Bitter Milk* I have argued that for both men and women, schooling presents a second chance to shape the subjectivity of their children, and belatedly, of themselves. Men, I have argued, contradict the inferential nature of paternity as well as the abstract value of their own masculinity by using the schooling and knowledge to claim their children, weaving family ties through name, class, property. Women, on the other hand, use schooling and curriculum to separate from children, gaining distance and autonomy for both themselves and their children by releasing the child to the surrogacy of the school and the logos of the fathers.

If schooling serves both men and women as a means to repudiate the constraints that they have experienced as biology, gender and culture have shaped their relations to their progeny, then it is reasonable to suspect that the male motive of identification and the female motive of differentiation would encourage both sexes to leave home home when they go to school. The denial that makes home disappear at the classroom door, becoming more and more distant as the grades go higher and higher, disassociates the experience of domestic work from the experience of work that school and wage labour supplies. It is ironic that at a time when the welfare of families has been severely undermined by the economy, managers are being prodded to adopt personnel policies and production protocols that resemble family groupings and collabourative work.

Metaphors Of Domestic Labour In Schools And Workplaces

Contemporary criticisms of the workplace have challenged the isolation of workers from the construction of policies concerning both process and product. Providing employee ownership of capital and profit sharing have been radical initiatives devised to give workers a stake in the work they do. Liberal solutions address the employee cohort, encouraging the creation of teams that encompass everyone involved with the invention, production and marketing of a cluster of related products. This agenda is developed by Robert B. Reich, in *Tales of a New America* around the concept of *collective entrepreneurship*.

This model of production requires relations of duration. Products are not dropped as soon as they are marketable but are continuously adapted and re-adapted as technologies and markets mature. Seeing production as a continuous process of reinvention, Reich argues that entrepreneurial efforts must be focussed on many thousands of small ideas rather than a few big ones:

> The point is that some form of employee ownership and control could provide a superior context for forging joint commitment and fostering trust. Reciprocal dependencies would be clearer. Relationships would be longer-term, and reputations correspondingly more important; the slacker and exploiter would bear the burden of their actions (Reich, 1988, 248).

> Individual skills are integrated into a group whose collective capacity to innovate becomes something more that the simple sum of its parts. Over time, as group members work through various problems and approaches together, they learn about each other's abilities. They learn how they can help one another perform better, who can contribute to what to a particular project, how they can best gain expertise together. Innovation is inherently collective and incremental (Reich, 1988, 124).

Is it merely coincidence that current curriculum approaches stress whole language literacy programs, the writing process, collabourative learning and peer tutoring, peer coaching and reciprocal teaching? Can it be that we have found the solution: that we now have devised a politics of instruction that will prepare students for active participation in a democratic workplace?

Reich declares that collective entrepreneurs will replace the triumphant individuals, the Carnegies, the Iococcas, who have been the heroes of American enterprise. He condemns the competitive individualism that offers achievement as a prize for industry that is isolated, self-motivated and autonomous. He argues that technology suffuses product development with so many possibilities that no one head man, no matter how creative and enterprising, can tame and guide its energies. But

Reich is unable to locate the resources that will feed the collective entrepreneurship he envisions. Haddad's research indicates that the the computer technologies Reich heralds as collaborative and interactive have not themselves engendered collaborative social organization in the workplace.

Whereas the information age was touted as a solution to the pink collar assembly lines that sunk workers in repetitive and fragmented tasks, Carole Haddad argues that computerization has not led to networking among workers but to their deskilling (1987, 42). She cites a Feldberg and Glaen study of the impact of technology on the work of customer service clerks in a utility company. Computers made it possible for a single worker to manage the tasks that had been performed previously by separate persons, but the breadth of the job was undermined by the surveillance that the computer program provided, accompanying each task with time frames, and continuously tabulating the volume of work and error rate of each worker.

Similar conclusions were reached by Barbara Garson in her scathing critique of technology in the workplace, *The Electric Sweatshop*. Her interviews of managers and cooks at McDonald's, reservation agents at American Airlines, social workers at a department of social services, yielded portraits of workers whose creativity, self-respect, sense of initiative, of character or flair were irrelevant to their employment in computerized industries (1989). The literature on computerization of the workplace is vast and these few examples cannot constitute an exhaustive study; nevertheless, few schools are equipped to offer better versions of information technology than the mechanistic systems that Garson describes. Investing heavily in personal computers with word processing capabilities, set up in rows in large carpeted enclosures, most schools and colleges have merely replicated the social relations of the insurance claims offices described above. Even the more interactive technologies such as laser and interactive videodisks, multimedia walls and virtual reality simulations, for all their fluidity, cannot change a school or workplace that has no social ethic for developing and sustaining human communities.

Now I am not going to nominate the family as a model for the collective entrepreneurship that Reich proposes. The duration of family relations can freeze members in infantalizing dependencies, defensive denials, debilitating jealousies, endless inadequacies, all grouped lovingly in a family portrait. Nevertheless, it is only against a ground of duration that any person can perceive both his or her own development as well as that of others.

In settings that discourage interaction, in work environments that encourage mobility and transience, the interpretation of one's own experience becomes a fiction with a new book for every chapter. When the setting and the characters are changing like a kaleidoscope, possibility seems to always hover in one more turn of the tube. Drenched in alternative actions, approaches, structures and roles, the mobile, flexible, individual worker does not become autonomous or interactive, merely anxious. The post modern metaphor of position expresses this manic mobility with the subject skittering around an endless parking lot, forever seeking the right spot.

Contemporary fascination with of school based management and shared decision making suggests this easy, and finally superficial process of change. Perched in a desert of bureaucratic governance, teachers have developed defensive responses to the cruel and gratuitous criticisms of schooling that government and private industry have generated to mask their own failures and limitations. Restructuring initiatives that invite teachers to be empowered by deliberating on the materials budget, but ignore the student teacher ratios are cruel jokes. Changing roles must be tied to changing the place itself and what it is about, or else so-called school reform is not worth the bother.

What domestic labour offers us is not a model for emulation but a shared text for interpretation. It is an enterprise directed toward care, sustained over time. It exists in physical time and space takes on a material presence that we all recognize, even though the sense we make of it may be different.

In her 1988 book, *In the Age of the Smart Machine: The Future of Work and Power*, Shoshana Zuboff suggests another model for information technology, one that enlarges the repertoires of workers, inviting their development instead of shutting it down.

According to Zuboff, the informated organization "textualizes" work. Traditionally, Western organizational theorists, from Frederick Taylor to Herbert Simon, have viewed the organization as a machine for collecting, processing, and disseminating information. In contrast, the learning organization is a group of workers gathered around a central core that is the electronic text. People take up their relationship toward that text according to their responsibilities and their information needs. In this context, work consists of the interpretation of data, in order to create meaning (Zuboff, 394).

The interpretation of shared texts is a learning process central to the teacher education programs at Brooklyn College. We initiate our programs with a studio course specifically designed to invite our students to recount their own educational experiences. We need to drop that cup once more, to remember our mother's rebuke in order to understand the insecurity that invites the people we care about to become so attached to objects. We need to think again about those brothers, two of them and no big help, and to recognize the ways that the chores we assumed supported their privilege and their infantalization. Our notions of family life are so thick with ideology, like the accretions that build up under the refrigerator (how often do you move the refrigerator?) we can barely see the ground. Together, students and faculty use these accounts of educational experience as a central text. A hermeneutic process such as Zuboff predicts and we employ recognizes that information requires interpretation, that the lines on the screen cannot be merely transferred, but that they must be interpolated with the responses, understandings and suggestions of a company of readers.

The interpretation of text is a path that I can mark, stretching from cradle to corporation. It suggests a way of work in an information age that directly draws upon the literacy of domesticity as well as schooling. It invites not only the understanding and communication of individuals but also the negotiation of alternatives that will produce a consensus sufficiently stable to sustain human society. I remain sceptical, however, when information technology diffuses the interpretive community in cluster organizations all over the place. These are defined as groups of people who work together to solve business problems or define a process and will then disband when the job is done. Team members may be geographically removed from one another; they may never have met. But telecommunication systems will enable those with complementary skills to work closely together.

This vision of far-flung collaboration may seem well suited to the current needs of families. By 1977 only 16% of American families matched the nuclear model that Parsons had celebrated in 1960 (Epstein, 1987). Yet we still shape public policy around the model of a full-time homemaker, caring for children by herself. Patterns of collaboration are everywhere: in domesticity, in extended families, in neighbourhood cooperatives, car pools, in shared jobs. Even within the putative nuclear family, the isolation of the mother has been mythologized. Psychologies of child development have been excessively dyadic, ignoring the adult world of concerns and commitments and attachments that framed the mother's life, and theorizing these attachments only as absence rather than presence in a child's experience. Friendships of women, extending over decades, have developed into communities of nurture for their children and their spouses.

Single parents are isolated in domiciles that discourage shared parenting and domesticity. Two-parent families also suffer from the needless replication of their labour. For years I would drive down my suburban street, exhausted by my hour's drive on the New York State Thruway, guilty that I was late, knowing that my pathetic gesture towards dinner would be rejected by tired kids already sated on snacks. Then I would wonder why the families who shared our street and our lives could never get together so that we could take turns cooking, picking up the kids, doing errands, getting the wash done. Oh, we helped each other out much of the time, but it always required arrangements, for we were working against the constant presumption of self-sufficiency.

It is little consolation to read Dolores Hayden's magnificent account of material feminism and of its struggle to socialize domestic labour by developing living spaces that would support communal kitchens, laundries, nurseries, appliances. Surviving on take-out, fast food, cleaners, laundries, and daycare, we have replicated the services that the material feminists envisioned without creating the communities to sustain them. Honouring the visions of Fourier and Olmsted, Marx and Engels, Bellamy and Gilman, Hayden reminds us that "it requires a spatial imagination to understand that urban regions designed for inequality cannot be changed by new roles in the lives of individuals" (1989, 28).

And so I doubt that the proliferation of computer screens disseminated around the country can provide the shared space that we need to constitute the spaces within which home, school and work can flourish. This is a lesson that domestic labour can teach us. We live in our bodies in time and space with other people. By now we should know that no technology can release us from the constraints of material necessity — clean air and water, space for thought as well as movement. If it was industry, as Hayden argues, that dominated homes by drawing factory workers out to the suburbs and into atomized dwellings, we should be warned and not let the industry of information technology further divide us.

NOTES:

1. This argument is elaborated in Chapter II of *Bitter Milk: Women and Teaching*, "Pedagogy for Patriarchy: The Feminization of Teaching."

2. In *Schoolgirl Fictions* (1990) Valerie Walkerdine identifies the bourgeois mother as the medium for regulation, a home economy that prepares the child for the obedience, muting of feeling and impulse that the society requires.

3. In *A Forest of Symbols* Victor Turner makes this point about anthropological studies of ritual. He argues that unless observations are taken over time, the anthropologist will fail to notice and understand the ways that rituals change over time as the political, economic and gender relations of the community are transformed, thus perceiving the rituals and the societies they signify as static.

References

Elson, Diane, and Pearson, Ruth (1991), "The subordination of women and the internationalisation of factory production," in Young, Kate, Wolkowitz, Carol and McCullagh, Roslyn (eds.), *Of marriage and the* market: women's subordination internationally and its lessons.* New York: Routledge, and Kegan Paul.

Epstein, Cynthia Fuchs (1988), *Deceptive distinctions: Sex, gender and the social order.* New Haven, Con.: Yale University Press.

Garson, Barbara (1989), *The electric sweatshop.* New York: Penguin.

Grumet, Madeleine R. (1988) *Bitter milk: women and teaching.* Amherst, Massachusetts: University of Massachusetts Press.

_____(1991), "Curriculum and the art of daily life," in George Willis and William Schubert (eds.), *Reflections from the heart of educational inquiry.* Albany, N.Y.: State University Press of New York.

Haddad, Carole J. (1987), "Technology, industrialization and the economic status of women," in Barbara Drygulski Wright (ed.), *Women, work and technology.* Ann Arbor, Mich.: University of Michigan Press.

Harris, Olivia. (1991), "Households as natural units," in Young, Kate,Wolkowitz, Carol and McCullagh, Roslyn (eds.), *Of marriage and the market: women's subordination internationally and its lessons.* New York: Routledge, and Kegan Paul.

Hayden, Dolores (1989), *The grand domestic revolution.* Cambridge, Mass.: The MIT Press.

Michie, Helen (1987), *The flesh made word: Female figures and women's bodies.* New York: Oxford University Press.

Reich, Robert B. (1988), *Tales of a new America.* New York: Vintage.

Turner, Victor, *A forest of symbols.* Ithaca, N.Y.: Cornell University Press.

Walkerdine, Valerie (1990), *Schoolgirl fictions.* London: Verso.

Woolf, Virginia (1927, 1955), *To the Lighthouse.* New York: Harcourt, Brace and World.

Zuboff, Shoshana (1988), *In the age of the smart machine: The future of work and power.* New York: Basic Books.

Chapter Seven

Subject To The New Global Economy
Power And Positioning In Ontario Labour Market Policy Formation

Kari Dehli
Ontario Institute for Studies in Education

Since the late 1970s thousands of Canadians have experienced the volatility of markets and industries once thought to be stable sources of work and income. Many analysts suggest that rapidly fluctuating demand in domestic and global markets can no longer be met within the context of mass production and the institutional relations associated with postwar Fordism and Keynesianism. Computer technology, knowledge-based production and flexible forms of organization, they argue, signal the arrival of a new "techno-economic paradigm."[1] The effects and significance of these shifts for workers, firms and communities in Canada are uneven.[2] For many it means dislocations, layoffs, casualization, lower wages and poorer working conditions, while for some it means improved job opportunities and increased salaries.[3]

While people experience and respond to restructuring in their workplaces, families and neighbourhoods, many issues must also be negotiated on the terrain of the state. As governments attempt to reduce deficits or establish new modes of regulating markets, social movements press for better protection for those whose lives and aspirations are being "adjusted." Such groups resist cut-backs; demand new state programs or increased funding for existing ones; work to change state institutions, programs and policies; and campaign to make governments extend and implement equity, affirmative action, human rights and anti-harassment legislation.

Here I am interested in one part of the response to "restructuring" in the Province of Ontario — current policy formation in the area of regulation and delivery of education and training for work. I will show that there is more at stake in struggles around training policies and programs than traditional approaches in political economy or policy research allow us to see. The key categories of political economy — class, mode of production, surplus value — as well as the theoretical innovations of the Regulation School — regime of accumulation, and mode of regulation — are useful in explaining transformations in capitalist social formations. However, they are not sufficient to explain the social organization of state policy responses to restructuring, or the meanings of different strategies adopted by people in their struggle to come to terms with "the new global economy."

In the midst of social and economic polarization and conflict in Canada, training and education for work have been depicted as an area of policy where social "partnerships" are possible and where consensus can, and must, be achieved. Moreover, politicians of diverse ideological stripes profess the conviction that the knowledge, skills and qualifications of present and future workers are critical to enhancing individual and collective prosperity.[4] Thus, soon after the Ontario New Democratic Party's election victory in September, 1990, Premier Bob Rae, sounding very much like his Liberal and Conservative predecessors, stated that the province's "competitive advantage is the quality of our schools, our infrastructure and our work force ... Ontario's future ... depends on a well-functioning partnership among government, business and labour."[5]

Many recent federal and provincial policy documents deal with education and training. Here I focus on the July 1990 report of the Ontario Premier's Council, *People and Skills in the New Global Economy*, and the events which followed its release. The Premier's Council recommended that a new policy-making and administrative structure for work-related training and adjustment, the Ontario Training and Adjustment Board (OTAB), be created. OTAB "would be a bipartite management and labour authority to provide strategic direction for the funding and delivery of workplace training and adjustment activities in the province."[6] The creation of the OTAB was endorsed by the NDP government soon after it was elected in September 1990. Speaking for the government in October 1990, Labour Minister Bob Mackenzie said that *People and Skills in the New Global Economy* "set a clear groundwork for the new government's thinking on labour adjustment programs."[7] Thus *People and Skills* provides a framework for discussing the issues involved in training and education debates, struggles around attempts to establish forms of social democratic policy processes, and discourses of social "partnership" in Ontario.[8]

While state efforts to establish new policy-making frameworks for training and education for work seek, at a very general level, to redefine relations between capital and labour, these relations are simultaneously reinforced, fragmented and interrupted by relations and politics of ethnicity, race, gender, sexuality and (dis)ability. Thus, attempts to frame policy initiatives solely in terms of the presumed requirements of "the new global economy" have been frustrated by interventions from unions and a range of social equity groups, who insist that social justice be incorporated into the training policy agenda. At the same time, the varied experiences and interests represented by these groups cannot be captured within traditional notions of class, or by focusing on politics at the point of production.

In order to understand how different groups are positioned and invested in contemporary training and education debates in Ontario, I draw on political economy and on theoretical work which incorporates understandings of the subject and the productive capacities of knowledge and discourse.[9] Current debates about, and research into training for work are seldom informed by an understanding of developments in the sociology of knowledge, critiques of epistemology and questions of the subject,[10] even though critical scholarship on education — from Marxist, feminist, anti-racist and poststructuralist perspectives — has flourished in the past 20 years. By and large, however, concern about vocational and technical education and workplace training has not been central to the endeavours of critical scholars.[11] One consequence of this is that much of the research being done — and the policy documents and debates which draw on it — has remained empiricist and functionalist, rarely questioning the relationship between education and "the needs of industry."[12]

The current "consensus" on skills training and education in Ontario is constructed around business demands for increased competitiveness, innovation and development on the one hand, and the arguments of labour and social activists that improved training and education can widen access to credentials and skills on the other. That is, training and education are thought capable of serving both economic and social ends, first by enhancing the qualifications of the labour force (hence improving competitiveness and the province's ability to attract investment), and second by providing avenues towards equity and employment opportunities for groups and individuals that have hitherto been relegated to low-paid and insecure jobs, or excluded from the labour market altogether.[13]

Investigating Labour Market Policy Formation

The form and language of policy texts in modern capitalist states draw us into ways of reading, speaking and thinking which are divorced from the everyday experiences of people whose lives or behaviour are constituted as policy problems.[14] It is important to see, however, that in our ordinary ways of making sense of our lives we take up policy (and other) discourses, whose frameworks and categories circulate through institutions such as the media, workplaces, schools and colleges. As documents authorized by government, based on "objective" knowledge and representing consensus among important "stakeholders," policy reports produce powerful truths about the world in which we live, work and learn. These truths have consequences, which are neither consistent nor determined beyond the contexts in which they are written and read.[15] Thus, reports such as *People and Skills in the New Global Economy* introduce and organize frameworks for thinking about and explaining the effects of economic change — in this case as matters of the deficiencies in knowledge and skills of workers in an increasingly competitive and aggressive world. Nevertheless, even as such explanations become pervasive, individuals and groups challenge dominant discourses and the power relations they reinforce and represent, producing and negotiating alternative and different understandings.[16]

As Dorothy Smith has argued, policy texts, and the practices through which they are produced and read, are "active" in that they intend particular frames for reading, and enable concerted and organized courses of action through a series of settings, such as government departments, parliament, academic institutions and the media.[17] Such documents are not windows into the realities or facts they describe; they are rather key constituents of the social relations which structure and organize those realities as factual. Smith shows how the discursive character of modern corporations and governments makes it possible for talk and action to be knitted together over time and across different sites, including, in this case, education and training institutions, union offices, women's groups and community organizations. Through discursive practices, local and particular experiences are re-presented and transformed into an extra-local "documentary reality," thus facilitating the social organization of management and regulation.

One of my aims is to explore the relations of power and knowledge through which *People and Skills* was produced, taken up and (later) struggled over. I link this exploration to theoretical debates about the subject, and the sociology of knowledge and discourse. First, I briefly trace how processes of policy formation, here the writing and circulation of *People and Skills*, transform people's experiences of work, economic upheaval and political struggle into administrative categories which can be put to work in state institutions and practices.

The questions here are of two types: First, what kind of framework does the report provide for understanding contemporary economic and social change? How are people's senses of who they are and what they know represented in the report. How are they positioned within (changing) market relations and the administrative and bureaucratic organization of labour market and training programs?[18] Second, how does the report construct particular subject positions and relations, so that few are positioned as knowers, speaking and acting in the interest of the social whole, while many are known and seen to constitute social problems, requiring regulation or intervention in the form of education and training? I ask how (different) knowing and working subjects are characterized and positioned in relation to each other, as well as how such characterizations and positionings construct "other" subject positions for those who do not quite fit the dominant schema and relationships.

Finally, I trace some of the political debates about recommendations in *People and Skills*, especially struggles over the Ontario Training and Adjustment Board since the NDP government was elected. Rather than achieving a consensus, the OTAB debates have opened up new terrains of political struggle in Ontario, particularly among groups on the broadly defined Left. The OTAB constructs a domain of labour market decision making regulated by, but at a distance from, the state. In this domain, I argue, particular modes of political representation and forms of political subjectivity are constituted.[19] Different political subject positions are being created for and by organizations representing employed workers, women, Native peoples, people of colour and people with disabilities. At the same time, the terms of their participation are contentious, often setting different groups against the state, each other and the people whose "interests" they seek to articulate.

I should point out that I take it as given that global economic restructuring is not merely or mainly a "technical" process. The ways in which people produce, regulate and define knowledge and skills, and the vastly different rewards and recognition accorded to the skills of different groups of people are political questions. Indeed, it is people rather than skills at the centre of contemporary changes in the global economy.

People And Skills In The New Global Economy: Constructing The Frame And Working Up The Categories

The Ontario Premier's Council on Technology was established in April 1986 by Premier David Peterson, who chaired its meetings and appointed the members. In addition to the Premier, four cabinet ministers attended the meetings. A large majority of the thirty-six member Council were corporate executives from firms such as IBM, Spar Aerospace, Northern Telecom and General Electric. Leo Gerard (Steelworkers), Fred Pomeroy (Communications and Electrical Workers) and Gordon Wilson (Ontario Federation of Labour) represented organized labour, while four university and college presidents, two heads of national research organizations and a school trustee spoke for the education sector. Only four members were women, fewer still came from visible minority groups.[20]

The Council's mandate was to "steer Ontario into the forefront of economic leadership and technological innovation."[21] In 1988 the Council issued volume one of its first report, *Competing in the New Global Economy*, with two additional volumes issued later in 1988 and in 1989. The Council's second report, *People and Skills in the New Global Economy*, came out just a few months before the provincial election in which the Liberal party was defeated by the NDP. In addition to producing these reports the Council also continues to fund union research and training projects, as well as research and development projects in corporations and post-secondary institutions.

People and Skills consists of three main sections, the titles of which suggest both the tone and orientation of the report: "Educating for the New Millennium," "Addressing the Training Deficit," and "Adjusting to Change." Here I am mainly interested in the middle section, which contains recommendations to set up the Ontario Training and Adjustment Board. The preface of the report establishes the credibility of the Council by identifying the range of "interests" represented among its members and the variety of groups and experts, with "a broad array of perspectives," consulted in the gathering of evidence. Further legitimacy is sought by pointing to the

Council's "lengthy deliberations" and frequent meetings, and by publicly acknowledging that there were areas where members did not agree. Employer and labour representatives differed over means "to increase the investment in training in industry," and especially over whether or not a payroll tax should be imposed on employers for this purpose.[22] In the end, a voluntary measure was proposed, with an option to introduce such a tax in the future.

Policy reports construct frameworks for making sense of the familiar and everyday world in which we live and work, and for orienting readers towards particular ways of seeing social problems and attendant solutions. *People and Skills* thus begins by describing a background of crisis and change, as do other recent reports on the state of the economy and labour market in Canada.[23] In the introduction we read that there are "signs that growth is faltering," that "production has fallen," that there are "slumping sales" and that previously strong sectors have "softened," prices have "dropped" and "giants are retrenching."[24] Facts are assembled from a variety of sources — industry studies, reports from other countries, meetings with "experts" — to produce this description and to develop a sophisticated analysis and a concerted strategy for change.

The report describes Ontario's postwar economy as one organized around resource extraction and standardized mass production for mass consumption. It argues (as do many other observers) that this type of production, characteristic of Fordism, will be unable to sustain past levels of prosperity. The pressures of increasingly globalized competition make change inevitable. Indeed, the report's "central message" is that:

> we cannot cling to low-wage, low value added activities where we have no competitive advantages, but must move into the high value-added, high-wage goods and services wherein lies our best hopes for prosperity over the long term. This shift will require continuing improvements in the productivity of both capital and labour.[25]

The Council recommends that government take an interventionist approach to ensure that "old" forms of production be replaced by diverse and "flexible" market and production relations, wherein small, "knowledge-based" firms, best equipped to succeed in the new global economy, will assume a central place.

From the outset we are invited to share a sense of crisis and urgency, but also an optimism that there are solutions. The crisis can be managed. The writers acknowledge the negative effects of restructuring, but argue that although some may attempt to resist change — for example, workers who "cling" to the only jobs they can get, no matter how low paid — they are not deserving of government support. Rather, government policies should aim to shift production from low to high-wage employment. In the international division of labour, the authors assume that "other" nations are better positioned to obtain a "competitive advantage" through low-wage and low value-added manufacturing. They have little to say about the fact that this "advantage" is achieved at the expense of foreign workers, often young women, toiling under extremely exploitive and dangerous conditions in plants owned by the very same multinational corporations pushing for "knowledge-based" production in Canada.[26] It is worth noting as well that the language of accommodation or resistance to the "new global economy," is infused with and made to work through gendered meanings. Those who oppose "adjustment" are described as timid and fearful, clinging to old ways and resisting change. They are contrasted with individuals who embrace change by being competitive, creative, assertive and flexible, accepting constant learning and change as a challenge.

While the writers recognize that predictions of future knowledge and skill requirements are problematic, they suggest that the province is suffering from a "training deficit" which can and must be corrected. Thus they write:

> Technological change can result in either more highly skilled or substantially deskilled jobs. By encouraging and investing in the continuous growth in the education and training of its people, Ontario can influence the outcomes of restructuring and technological change to achieve more skilled and rewarding work for those affected by these phenomena.[27]

General characteristics and trends in the present are used to assert a need for increased investment and change in training and education for the future. Most of the investment to correct the "training deficit" would have to come from individuals or governments, as there are no recommendations to compel capital to invest in worker qualification.

The authors take great care to define skill. Their broad definition includes:

> all those acquired abilities that enable people to function effectively in their social and economic systems. These include not only the ability to perform tasks, but also the responsibility and judgment to perform them well. Basic skills include achievements like the ability to read or use numbers. Higher order technical skills might include abilities in engineering and science. There is also a range of occupation-related skills, such as welding or computer programming, and broad business or organizational abilities, such as managing, selling or negotiating.[28]

They construct a pyramid model in which different types of skill are grouped on three levels: basic skills at the bottom, portable workplace or higher-order skills in the middle, and non-portable firm and job-specific skills at the top. The model assumes that the skills and knowledges of individuals are acquired in a cumulative fashion, that there is a relatively linear and continuous set of steps from the basic to the more complex or advanced skills. At the same time, the pyramid is a visual representation of a distribution of people across various "levels" of skills and knowledge: the greatest number at its base, and few at the pinnacle. This model, in turn, provides a frame for allocating public, individual and employer responsibilities for the provision or acquisition of different levels of knowledge and skill: from elementary and secondary school, to apprenticeship or post-secondary education, and finally, firm-specific or workplace training.

This is a thoroughly rational model, devised as though people are equally able to move through education and training programs in an orderly and predictable fashion, and as though production relations comprise the sole context in which people take up vocational learning. Looking directly at the experiences of workers, students and trainees, however, the authors find that there are many who do not fit their model. Yet, rather than taking this as an indication that the model may be flawed, the authors search for common characteristics among those whose experiences and behaviour differ from their implicit norm: thus female gender, old age, non-Anglo-Saxon ethnicity, non-whiteness, unequal citizenship status, physical or mental disability come to be seen as "variables" determining degrees of disadvantage and difference in relation to a path by which "workers" ordinarily acquire knowledges or skills. The referent of the category "ordinary worker" remains young, Anglo-Saxon, white, Canadian-born and able-bodied males living in Southern Ontario, despite the fact that this group comprises a minority of current and future workers.

Historically, skill has constituted a site of negotiation and struggle between employers and workers, as well as among groups of workers and would-be workers, trainers, educators and policy makers. Within Western capitalist social formations, those jobs traditionally seen to involve skill and rewarded accordingly have been the preserve of white, male workers, who individually and through unions have gone to great lengths to exclude women and minorities.[29] Thus, the acquisition and meanings of skill, and its recognition, deployment and remuneration in the workplace are not as straightforward as the Premier's Council suggests.

Some firms and sectors in Canada have begun to require college or high school diplomas for entry-level jobs simply as a selection device. Likewise, completion of company-sponsored courses influences decisions about job assignments, promotions and wage-steps, even though such courses often have more to do with "company culture" than with job content or performance. In other cases, training is used as a method of selecting those who will retain their jobs during layoffs, even though courses may be offered in the evenings or on weekends with no provision for childcare, thus making them inaccessible to women who continue to perform a disproportionate share of childrearing and domestic labour.

In the terms of the Regulation School theorists, we could say that *People and Skills* aims to put in place new modes of regulating the institutions and processes which socialize and qualify labour power in Ontario.[30] The report argues that more people must be drawn into education and training, and that they must continue to retrain and educate themselves throughout their lifetime. Demands to improve worker qualification are linked to the requirements of computer technology, specialized forms of production and more flexible, team-oriented models of work organization. But the report does not analyze the specific and different social relations in which qualifications are acquired, nor the contexts in which individuals or firms take up training and education.[31] Other researchers have found that contemporary changes in the nature of workers' qualifications and the ways in which they are obtained, have an uneven and unpredictable impact on the social relations among workers and between workers and management, potentially undermining seniority rights and negotiated job classifications, and often increasing stress, anxiety and individual competitiveness.[32]

The Premier's Council is unable to address these problems because it deals with skill and equity as separate issues, in separate parts of the report. Although they do recognize that struggles over definitions and recognition of skill are endemic to capitalist production relations, the authors' pyramid model locates "skill" as a set of observable properties of jobs or individual workers. This reification of skill undermines the insight that questions of knowledge, qualification and competence are contentious and political. At the same time it reinforces the assumption that training and education programs comprise an instrumental system that can be shaped so as to meet both economic and equity objectives, by adjusting it to "the needs of industry" and by removing some of the discriminatory barriers within it. In responding to the report, the Advocates for Community-based Training and Education for Women (ACTEW) warned that the "belief ... that market forces will match up traditionally disadvantaged and discriminated against individuals with training and employment opportunities demanded by the economic restructuring" was "naive."[33] Along with ACTEW, many feminists in Canada and elsewhere argue that skill can most usefully be seen as a constituent of social relations, intimately linked to class, racial and gender divisions of paid and unpaid labour.[34] Struggles over skill and equity in workplace training and education programs are therefore inseparable.

Creating Subject Positions In Policy Texts

The features of policy formation which construct interpretive frames and organize bureaucratic action are different from, although related to, those which explicitly address "social problems" and the people who experience them, or whose behaviours or "deficiencies" are thought to be problematic. It is common to both, however, that practices of policy production and circulation establish, affirm or change different subject positions and their relation to each other. In *People and Skills* the key problem is a perceived lack of skills among current and future workers and the inadequate efforts to make up for what the authors call the "training deficit." The people whose lives and work are organized or disorganized through current upheavals in capitalist economies are not themselves present as knowers or active subjects in the text or in its making. Recent debates about skills and knowledge in this and similar reports position a narrow range of people as knowers who can frame questions and provide answers, theories and explanations, and as active subjects who can make things happen in social, economic and political organizations.

Even when policy recommendations are not implemented, reports such as those of the Premier's Council work in and beyond the different settings where they are read and discussed. Although ostensibly circulated for discussion among the "general public," the majority of readers of policy documents are members of specialist communities of some sort: journalists, politicians, bureaucrats or academics, teachers and education administrators, and activists of social movements and labour organizations. Newspapers print stories about policy documents, organizations debate them and pass resolutions, bureaucrats decide how to comply, academics write papers for conferences or journals. These specialist communities are the active subjects of policy discourse. The reading and discussion of policy documents are practices whereby such subjects are discursively positioned as doers and knowers. *People and*

Skills makes available positions from which certain groups or individuals can know and speak as "business," "labour" or "government." At the same time, the report provides a "resource through which speakers and hearers can negotiate new positions."[35] In other words, the report helps shape a ground on which collective social subjects — or rather the representatives of such collectivities who are conferred legitimacy through the very policy-forming processes in which they participate — can affirm old, or negotiate new, positions from which to speak and act.

Jacques Donzelot has argued that, across Western capitalist states, policy emphases on continuous training of the workforce since the late 1970s, can be linked to attempts to "break down the growing separation between the domain of social benefits and that of production."[36] He suggests that governments have adopted a range of strategies to transform postwar relations between individuals and the state. In the past, entitlements to benefits, such as pensions or unemployment insurance, were independent of levels of individual competence or national productivity. Now, he argues, a shift is underway from practices and discourses of citizens' statutory entitlements to programs and policies which appeal to "the adaptive autonomy of the individual." The Canadian government's reforms of unemployment insurance can be seen as a specific step in this direction, while appeals for individuals to "adjust" themselves to economic insecurity within global competitiveness constitute a more general indication. In practice, the shifts are not quite so sharp, however, and different and competing practices and relations continue to exist. The previous discussion of tensions between discourses and politics of skill and equity provides one example of this. Another instance is apparent in the labour market and training strategies of the Canadian and Ontario governments, whose positions regarding the level and form of state intervention, and the meanings attributed to the notion of a "training culture" are distinctly different.

People and Skills places lifelong learning and accessible training within a frame of global economic competitiveness. "The training culture" is described in a language of rights *and* in terms of the individual's responsibility to "adjust" to restructuring. The report criticizes the federal government's overall labour market policy direction, its withdrawal of funds from labour market programs and its move towards fragmented, short-term and privatized solutions. Comparing Canada (and pre-Liberal Ontario) unfavourably with other industrialized countries, the Council notes:

> Because labour market policy has focused on short-term income maintenance to tide people over until they can find a job, the current system does little to provide workers with the level of ongoing skills development needed to facilitate adjustment during periods of economic restructuring.[37]

While the federal government has shifted emphasis from programs targeted to specific populations — programs which, however inadequately, provided some sort of right to training or education for so-called equity groups — to ones which explicitly "meet the needs of industry," the Council proposes that Ontario develop long-term and proactive strategies that would give priority to high-skill training and employment, and alter regulations in areas such as lay-off notice and severance pay.

Since the release of the report, disagreements between the two levels of government have not been resolved. At the same time many training programs and entitlements to income support are being eroded, while complicated access criteria and long waiting lists make it difficult to enrol in others. Ironically, it is becoming harder to obtain formal credentials for those who are told they need them most: funding has been reduced, or eligibility criteria changed, for programs serving women who are (re-)entering the workforce, recent citizens and visible minority workers. Thus arguments between different levels of government about jurisdiction and organization of programs, as well as funding cuts, make it increasingly difficult for large numbers of people to take up "new" subject positions as skilled, knowledgeable workers. These discrepancies and tensions are among the key issues in struggles and negotiations to constitute "partnership" in training and labour market policy making.

State Formation, Social Movements And Politics Of "Partnership"

Fact-finding, consultation and report-writing are ordinary features of the work of policy making. In a paper on commissions of inquiry, Adam Ashforth argues that they confirm the state as collector and guarantor of social facts; as the proper convener of and referee among social "interests"; and as the regulator or organizer of appropriate "interventions".[38] Practices of policy formation negotiate, confirm or shift notions of what the state is and does, while the state's subjects are offered a range of positions from which to speak and act.[39] While Ashforth's interest is in the organization of commissions as a particular state form, I will focus on how subjects "act up" and struggle over state formation, over representation and over ways and means of exercising or resisting political authority.

New forms of regulation and rule were proposed by the Premier's Council: areas of decision making and administration are (apparently) transferred out of the direct domain of state power. While defining and investigating economic relations in general and the qualification of labour in particular, the Council sought to constitute policy and program mechanisms which could draw representatives of organized capital and labour into decision making in the area of labour market policy. The Council recommended that a more permanent policy-making institution, the Ontario Training and Adjustment Board, be set up at arm's length from the state. The OTAB would be a forum where representatives of capital, labour and the state could formulate and express "interests" in relation to education and training, while at the same time participating in the regulation and management of these domains.

The OTAB would regulate all provision of work-related training and adjustment programs in Ontario. Programs administered by ministries such as Labour and Skills Development would be transferred to the OTAB, as would several sectoral training initiatives in steel, automotive, electronic and electrical industries. It was initially intended to be a bipartite structure, with an equal number of seats for business and labour and ex-officio participation of key provincial and federal government ministries, but representation was widened to include four voting members who would be "general representatives ... selected on the recommendation and mutual approval of the management and labour members."[40] Since early 1991 state officials and representatives of several "stakeholder" groups have tried to agree on a model and mandate for OTAB. A consultation paper was finally issued in November 1991, entitled "Skills to Meet the Challenge: A Training Partnership for Ontario." A second paper on the composition and mandate of local training and adjustment boards was issued shortly thereafter, in collaboration with the Canadian Labour Market Development Board. Consultation meetings were held across the province in the spring of 1992. Although a secretariat is in place, the board itself has yet to be established. The target date for launching the OTAB has been changed several times and is now set for early 1993.

The composition, mandate and structure of the OTAB continue to be hotly contested among labour and social movement activists, representatives of business, state bureaucrats and provincial politicians. At stake in these negotiations between employers, the labour movement, social movements and government are the means to change and regulate the province's labour market, and especially the institutions and procedures through which workers' qualifications are acquired, recognized, differentiated, rewarded and controlled. The fact that a social democratic-led government, unions, labour federations, social equity groups and business have agreed to participate in these boards does not mean that there is unanimity within or among such organizations.[41] Far from being the one area where consensus can be reached and new social partnerships forged, training and education for work have turned out to be one of several contentious arenas of struggle in the province of Ontario.[42] At a recent (November, 1992) meeting, for example, labour and community activists who have been involved in the process of creating OTAB expressed frustration that business representatives, and the organizations they represent, continue to stall negotiations by changing their position or introducing new demands. One area of difference concerns whether, and how strongly, OTAB should insist that training programs be delivered by publicly-funded and accountable institutions. The wording of OTAB's overall mandate is yet another.

Two of the early questions of debate were whether or not to impose a training levy on employers, and whether and how the Board's mandate could include programs for people who are not employed, or employed in economically marginal sectors. The early OTAB model was consistent with the Council's attempt to use training as an active tool in economic restructuring, rather than targeting such programs to particular populations. This meant that the OTAB's programs would focus on services and industries in "traded" (i.e. export-oriented) sectors with competitive potential, and on employed workers in those sectors, or workers who could be trained to transfer there. Thus, programs designed for women, recent immigrants, members of visible minority groups, Native people, francophones and people with disabilities were excluded from or marginalized within the Premier's Council's proposals. Unless they were oriented to "traded" sector employment, such programs would remain a federal responsibility (usually falling under the Canadian Jobs Strategy) or the responsibility of other provincial ministries.

The Ontario Federation of Labour and the NDP government initially endorsed this separation. At the same time the OFL insisted that a training levy be imposed on employers, so as to prevent a "milking" of funds from equity-oriented programs to pay for workplace training.[43] The NDP government did not endorse an employer training levy, nor did it support legislation that would mandate employers to train workers or participate in industrial adjustment programs. Nevertheless, the mandate and membership of the proposed OTAB has been expanded, so as to include a broad range of training and education programs, as well as covering unemployed workers and people on social assistance. The current proposals for regarding OTAB's composition (released in the fall of 1992) include not only business and labour members, but also two representatives of the education sector and one representative each of Native people, visible minorities, the disabled, women, and francophones. Francophones were added following public consultations in the spring of 1992.

Many would argue that this representation is inadequate and

that the naming of some groups as representing social equity interests is contradictory. While it is crucial that women, Native people, visible minorities, the disabled and francophones choose their own representatives, their marginality from, or discrimination in, paid employment or training could be reinforced by organizing their labour market "interests" solely in terms of equity. The needs of people whom the equity groups are meant to represent are diverse, as are their relations to, and experiences in, education and employment. In contrast to such diversity, OTAB's representational model assumes coherent, resourceful and well-organized constituencies with unitary interests in training and education.

What the active presence of "others" in these debates also shows is that neither "business" nor "labour" can speak for all workers and non-workers in Ontario. Women, visible minorities, Native people, francophones and the disabled demand a right to speak for themselves: they demand to be granted political subjectivity in their own right, and they choose different organizational forms and modes of representation to claim that right. Indeed, the very presence of these groups (from among the many that could be seen to form constituencies with an interest in labour market and training questions) in the OTAB discussions is the result of many years of political organizing against sexism and racism in workplaces, unions and communities, for francophone rights and Native self-government and for self-determination and participation by people with disabilities. The claims of these groups, in terms of labour market training, thus arise from very different kinds of struggles for representation and community control. Their programs and their policy proposals have in common that they begin with an experiential knowledge of the interests and circumstances of men and women who will take part in training and education programs. Thus, training programs designed by and for women organize activities around child-care needs, and place as much emphasis on individual and collective strategies to question and combat sexism and racism in local communities, families and workplaces as they do on technical skills. Community literacy programs draw on the experience and knowledge of participants to develop curriculum, while integrating literacy learning with community development and advocacy. Although not entirely divorced from labour market requirements, these programs are not framed in terms of meeting "the needs of industry."[44] Activists in these programs are caught in a double bind: if their programs are excluded from the domain of OTAB, they fear that a two-tier system of training will develop, where priority will be given to those sectors and workers who have traditionally formed the core of the labour force. At the same time, they worry that inclusion within the framework of OTAB will mean that the quality and standards of all programs will be measured against narrowly defined objectives, with equity and developmental issues becoming secondary.

While there is good reason to be cautious about OTAB's ability to shape labour market and training policies and programs in progressive ways, many union and social equity activists agree that the OTAB initiative has succeeded in bringing together groups who had not worked together in the past, such as Advocates for Community based Training and Education for Women (ACTEW), Coalition of Visible Minority Women (Ontario), Ontario Council of Agencies Serving Immigrants (OCASI), and Ontario Literacy Coalition (OLC), to mention some. In turn, activists in these organizations have had numerous meetings with education and training activists in unions and the Ontario Federation of Labour, mostly at the staff level. Members of these coalitions include people who have several years' grassroots experience in providing or participating in community-based training and education programs. Many work in small non-profit, learner-centred programs that have grown out of, and are directed by, specific constituencies, such as immigrant women or tenants in public housing projects.

As social equity groups and unions in Ontario become more involved in training and adjustment debates and policy making, they continue to critique the assumptions which frame these debates and policies, and to link progressive agendas for training and education to questions of economic and industrial policy, job creation, full employment, social equity and social justice.[45] Unions have consistently argued that training must be a right and that it must be developmental rather than instrumental. Activists in women's groups insist that community development and job creation must be an integral part of training, and that equity objectives must be built into programs from the outset. At the same time, they have been able to obtain resources to enable marginalized groups to organize around training and education issues, so as to turn the "event" of the new training structures into an opportunity for mobilization and education.[46]

Arriving at a consensus among unions and social equity groups, however, has not always been straightforward. For example, unions initially made a strong case for coordinating all Ontario programs for work-related training through community colleges, as a way of defending publicly-funded and accountable educational institutions against privatization. Within a political economy framework, it may seem contrary to working class interests that many groups representing women, immigrant workers and people of colour resisted this position. While supporting community colleges and opposing privatization, these groups have argued that community based and accountable, non-profit education and training programs comprise a vital part of any strategy for change in education and training, and for linking such programs to community and economic development. They have argued, and the OFL now seems to agree, that a range of publicly-funded and accountable training and education programs are needed, and that the provincial government must continue to support both colleges and non-profit programs that are designed by and for specific communities, especially in light of federal government cutbacks and privatization strategies. This example suggests that the current politics of "restructuring" articulate complex investments and positions within and beyond the politics of production and economistic notions of class, whose expression and effects cannot be "read off" from such general notions as "post-Fordism" or "new techno-economic paradigms." Rather, they must be understood through particular and local investigations, where attention to political economy is but one concern.

Conclusions

The institutional practices and discursive forms through which policy documents constitute knowledge are implicated in and constituents of social relations of class, gender, race and ethnicity. They also produce conflicting subject positions, although the manner in which subject positions come to be taken up, or "embodied," is not given in advance. Thus, I have tried to consider both the textual organization of policy making and some of the practices involved in interpreting, negotiating and subverting the meanings of policy and practices of "implementation." In Ontario, organizations constituted around social categories such as labour, women, visible minorities, Native people, francophones and the disabled, have been invited to participate along with representatives of capital in a new "partnership," responsible for labour market and training policy. As these groups attempt to articulate alternate positions and understandings of the politics of training, they shape new forms of political subjectivity. These cannot necessarily be "read off" from texts such as the Premier's Council reports, nor predicted from general economic analyses.

I have only touched on a few aspects of the Premier's Council 1990 report, saying little about its many important recommendations regarding primary and secondary education, community colleges or universities, provisions for lay-off notices, and so on. I have tried, rather, to draw attention to how the work of the Ontario Premier's Council, and especially its 1990 report, *People and Skills*, continues to frame the formation of policy responses to economic restructuring in Ontario. The Council has not only contributed to political and policy debates on the issues it explicitly addresses, such as programs and policies to develop the knowledge and skills of workers, it has also helped to construct frames for making sense of these issues and for thinking about how to address them. The NDP government has continued the Council's attempts to create structures and discursive frameworks wherein different labour market "interests" can be represented, and where particular forms of knowledge can be produced, circulated and given legitimacy.

Some authors have argued that the crisis of Fordist forms of capitalist accumulation beginning in the 1970s, constitutes a crisis in political and institutional modes of representation and regulation as well as a crisis in production relations and the labour process.[47] The proposed political structures, policy frameworks and forms of knowledge produced by the Premier's Council are not entirely new nor particular to Ontario. We could view them as local responses to global transformations in relations between nation states, regional governments and increasingly integrated forms of capitalist production. The regulation, reproduction and qualification of labour power have gained renewed importance in state policy strategies in Western Europe and North America, as advanced industrial countries and regions compete to attract and hold the investment of corporations with "no fixed address."[48] The Premier's Council's emphasis on education and training of workers can thus be seen as one attempt to "market" the province to global capital as an attractive place to invest on the basis of its highly qualified (and thus, presumably highly productive) labour force.

At the same time, the Council's reports have contributed to the creation of new institutional structures and practices within the province, through which the politics of labour market policy can be spoken, and political and economic "interests" can be constituted and represented in new ways. This constitutes a shift in notions of what the state is and does, as well as how political subjectivity can be articulated and organized. Given its objective of regulating labour market and training initiatives, the OTAB could signal changes to state forms and political representation in late capitalist Ontario. Although the responsibility for policy direction will remain with government, the OTAB will establish agencies and practices, apparently outside the state, where labour market problems and needs can be identified and collectively managed by representatives of capital, labour, equity groups and state officials.

I have tried to show that the shape and content of these shifts, and the different investments of groups and individuals in them, cannot be predicted or "read off" from a general analysis of trends in the global economy. My criticism of *People and Skills in the New Global Economy* and of the proposed Ontario Training and Adjustment Board, is not that they are smokescreens which hide devious intentions, such as budget cuts, withdrawal of welfare entitlements or even more sinister attacks on working people, although these may be among their outcomes. Nor have I attempted to develop an alternative agenda for training which the NDP government could adopt. Instead I have tried to show how the Premier's Council does a particular kind of epistemological and political work, creating rationales for changes in labour market policy formation, and in modes of regulating education and training for future and incumbent workers. Although it is not surprising that a policy-making body should attempt to do this, it is important to explore the different ways in which a social democratic government, activists in unions, equity groups and social movements have taken up the discourse in which the Council was embedded, and the forms of representation that it proposed.

The debates around the Council's reports, and particularly its recommendations to establish a training and adjustment board, are not just arguments for or against a set of programs and structures. By participating in debates, organizing forms of representation, and publicly treating training and education as political and conflictual matters, new domains of political struggle and different political subject positions are being constituted. It remains to be seen, however, whether this process of constituting new subject positions within domains of public policy making will benefit the thousands of people who are living the overwhelmingly negative effects of restructuring.

NOTES:

Research for this paper was funded by a Post Doctoral Fellowship from SSHRC. I presented an earlier version to the Canadian Sociology and Anthropology Association meeting in Kingston in 1991. I am grateful for Leon Muszynski's critical comments as discussant in that session. I received valuable suggestions from the Learning-Skills-Work Seminar Group at OISE and from participants in the Transition from School to Work Seminars in Toronto and London. Pramila Aggarwal, Linzi Manicom, Alice de Wolff, Nancy Jackson, Susan Heald, Jenny Horsman, K. Judith Millen, Judith Marshall, Rianne Mahon, Ananda Kodikara, Jennifer Stephen and Marcy Cohen offered constructive criticisms, as did three SPE reviewers.

1. For different accounts and explanations, see M. Piore and C. Sabel, *The Second Industrial Divide: Possibilities for Prosperity* (New York: Basic Books, 1984); D. Wolfe, "Capitalist Crisis and Marxist Theory,"*Labour/Le*

Travail 17 (Spring, 1986), pp. 225–254; A. Lipietz, "Towards Global Fordism?" *New Left Review* 132 (March-April, 1982), pp. 33–47; F. Frobel, J. Heinrichs and Otto Kreye, *The New International Division of Labour* (Cambridge, Mass.: Cambridge University Press, 1980).

2. See several articles in D. Drache and M. S. Gertler (eds.), *The New Era of Global Competition: State Policy and Market Power* (Montreal and Kingston: McGill-Queen's University Press, 1991); and Jane Jenson, "'Different' but not 'Exceptional': Canada's Permeable Fordism" *Canadian Review of Sociology and Anthropology* 26/1 (1989), pp. 69–94.

3. G. Betcherman, *Good Jobs, Bad Jobs. Employment in the Service Sector* (Ottawa: Economic Council of Canada, 1990); J. Holmes, "The Globalization of Production and the Future of Canada's Mature Industries: The Case of the Automotive Industry," and A. Masi, "Structural Adjustment and Technological Change in the Canadian Steel Industry, 1970–1986"; both in Drache and Gertler, *The New Era of Global Competition*; and Peter Warrian, "Industrial Restructuring, Occupational Shifts and Skills: The Steel and Manufacturing Cases," in Ontario Council of Regents, *Colleges and the Changing Economy. Background Papers, Visions 2000* (Toronto, 1989).

4. For a critique, see Nancy S. Jackson, "Skill Training in Transition: Implications for Women," in Jane S. Gaskell and Arlene Tigar McLaren (eds.), *Women and Education: A Canadian Perspective* (Calgary: Detselig, 1987).

5. "Rae to boost training, hi-tech," *The Toronto Star* 19 October, 1991, p. C1; See also The Ontario Training and Adjustment Board, *Skills to Meet the Challenge: A Training Partnership for Ontario* (Toronto: The Queen's Printer for Ontario, 1991); Margot Gibb-Clark, "Improved Training of Staff Becoming Essential Tool," *The Globe and Mail* 23 January, 1990; David Crane, "Growth in Skilled Workers Vital for '90s, Report Says," *The Toronto Star* 26 May, 1990.

6. The Premier's Council, *People and Skills In the New Global Economy* (Toronto: Queen's Printer for Ontario, 1990).

7. Quoted in "Ontario plans major reforms to help tide of jobless workers," *The Financial Post* 11 October, 1990.

8. *People and Skills*, p. 140.

9. Among many contributions, see Michel Foucault, *The History of Sexuality, Volume I: An Introduction*, trans. Robert Hurely (New York: Vintage/Random house, 1980); *idem, Power-Knowledge*, ed. Colin Gordon (London: Harvester 1980); and Carolyn Ellis and Michael G. Flaherty (eds.), *Investigating Subjectivity. Research on Lived Experience* (Newbury Park: Sage, 1992).

10. But see, Jacques Donzelot, "Pleasure in Work," in Graham Burchell, Colin Gordon and Peter Miller (eds.), *The Foucault Effect: Studies in Governmentality* (Chicago: University of Chicago Press, 1991).

11. See Jackson, "Skill Training in Transition." It is worth noting that sever-

al Canadian researchers of vocational education and training for work are among those who do incorporate recent debates in social theory into their inquiries, albeit in very different ways. See the work of Marcy Cohen, Nancy Jackson, David Livingstone, Roger Simon, Dorothy Smith and George Smith.

12. Jackson, "Skill Training in Transition..." p. 351.

13. Rianne Mahon, "Toward a Highly Qualified Workforce: Improving the Terms of the Equity-efficiency Trade-off," in Ontario Council of Regents, *Colleges and the Changing Economy*....

14. Dorothy E. Smith, *The Conceptual Practices of Power: A Feminist Sociology of Knowledge* (Toronto: University of Toronto Press, 1990).

15. Adam Ashforth "Reckoning Schemes of Legitimation: On Commissions of Inquiry as Power/Knowledge Forms," *Journal of Historical Sociology* 3/1 (March, 1990).

16. See Jennifer Stephen, "Progressive Disease," *This Magazine* 26/3 (September, 1992), pp. 28–30.

17. Dorothy Smith, "Textually Mediated Social Organization," *International Social Science Journal* 36/1 (1984).

18. My analysis of these questions draws on Patricia Morgan, "From Battered Wife to Program Client: The State's Shaping of Social Programs," *Kapitalistate* 9 (1981); and Gillian Walker, "The Conceptual Politics of Struggle: Wife Battering, the Women's Movement, and the State," *Studies in Political Economy* 33 (Autumn, 1990).

19. Marcy Cohen is exploring some of these questions in her work with the Canadian Labour Force Development Board. "Presentation to the Panel on Training Strategies," Learned Societies Meeting, Charlottetown, PEI, May 31, 1992.

20. *People and Skills*, pp. v-vi. While the Premier's Council itself had only three members (out of a total of 35) who explicitly represented organized labour when this report was written, a significant group of academics, labour and education activists identified with the political left were involved in writing different parts of the report, see Appendix A, p. 215. Others were members of, or made presentations to, Council subcommittees. Appendix C lists members of the three sub-committees (education, skills training and labour adjustment) as well as the people who made presentations to them (pp. 217–222).

21. The Premier's Council, *Competing in the New Global Economy* (Toronto: Queen's Printer for Ontario, 1988), p. 5.

22. *People and Skills*, p. 1.

23. Ontario Council of Regents, *Colleges and the Changing Economy*...; Canadian Labour Market and Productivity Centre, *Report of the CLMPC Task Forces on the Labour Force Development Strategy* (Ottawa: The Cen-

tre, 1990) and CLMPC, *A Framework for a National Training Board the Report of the Phase II Committee on the Labour Force Development Strategy* (Ottawa: The Centre, 1990).

24. *People and Skills*, p.1.

25. *People and Skills*, p.1.

26. See Swasti Mitter, *Common Fate, Common Bond. Women in the Global Economy* (London: Pluto Press, 1986); Gita Sen and Caren Grown, *Development, Crises and Alternative Visions. Third World Women's Perspectives* (New York: Monthly Review Press, 1987); Diane Elson and Ruth Pearson, "Third World Manufacturing," in *Waged Work A Reader* (London: Verso, 1986) [A collection of papers from Feminist Review]; Cynthia Enloe, *Bananas, Beaches and Bases. Making Feminist Sense of International Politics* (London: Pandora, 1989); Kathryn Ward (ed.), *Women Workers and Global Restructuring* (Ithaca, N.Y.: ILR Press, 1990).

27. *People and Skills*, p. 4.

28. *People and Skills*, pp. 4–5.

29. Cynthia Cockburn, *Brothers. Male Dominance and Technological Change* (London: Pluto Press, 1983); Anne Phillips and Barbara Taylor, "Sex and Skill," and Amina Mama, "Black Women and the Economic Crisis," both in *Waged Work. A Reader*...; Ann Wickham, *Women and Training* (Milton Keynes: Open University Press, 1986).

30. Michel Aglietta, *A Theory of Capitalist Regulation* (London: New Left Books, 1979); Alain Lipietz, *Mirages and Miracles* (London: Verso 1987).

31. Dorothy E. Smith suggests that this is a typical feature of training policy texts, see "Training Implications of New and Old Techno-economic Paradigms in the Plastics Processing Industry: The Managerial Experience," unpublished paper, Ontario Institute for Studies in Education, 1990.

32. Phillipe Mehaut, "New Firms' Training Policies and Changes in the Wage-earning Relationship," *Labour and Society* 13/4 (October, 1988); David Robertson and Jeff Wareham, *Technological Change in the Auto Industry* (North York: CAW Technology Project, February, 1987).

33. Advocates for Community Based Training and Education for Women, "A Community Based Response to the Premier's Council Report: 'People and Skills in the New Global Economy'" (Toronto: ACTEW, December, 1990). While ACTEW has been one of the most outspoken critics of the Premier's Council, their position has been endorsed by several groups, such as the Ontario Literacy Coalition and the City of Toronto's Workers' Action and Information Centre.

34. Phillips and Taylor, "Sex and Skill..."; Dorothy Smith, "Training Implications..."; and Nancy Jackson, "Skill Training in Transition...".

35. Bronwyn Davis and Rom Harre, "Positioning: the Discursive Production of Selves," *Journal for the Theory of Social Behaviour* 20/1 (1990).

36. Donzelot, "Pleasure in Work," p. 272.

37. *People and Skills*, p. 108.

38. Ashforth "Reckoning Schemes..."

39. Philip Corrigan and Derek Sayer, *The Great Arch. English State Formation as Cultural Revolution* (Oxford: Basil Blackwell 1985).

40. *People and Skills*, pp. 141–142.

41. For example, the Ontario Federation of Labour and the Canadian Manufacturing Association have taken different positions on questions of privatization of training and implementation of a training tax on employers. See "Education and Training," policy paper adopted at the 33rd Annual Convention of the Ontario Federation of Labour, Toronto, November 20–24, 1989. Within the labour movement the Canadian Auto Workers and the Communications and Electrical Workers of Canada have taken quite different positions on joint labour-management participation in training decisions, as well how unions should respond to workplace reorganization and introduction of new technology. Compare an undated paper by CAW researchers Sam Gindin and David Robertson, "Democracy and Productive Capacity. Notes Towards and Alternative to Competitiveness" with Communications and Electrical Workers of Canada, "An Agenda for the Future. CWC's Position on Workplace Reorganization," policy paper adopted at the 7th Annual Convention, Quebec, May 7–11, 1991.

42. See David Robertson, "Contrasting Agendas: Building a Training System," Text based on presentation to the Premier's Council Subcommittee on Training, Toronto, 8 September, 1987.

43. Ontario Federation of Labour, "The Report of the Premier's Council on Education, Training and Adjustment," OFL Press Release, Toronto, July 25, 1990; OFL, "Report to the OFL Education Committee from OFL Training Subcommittee," OFL document, March 12, 1991.

44. These observations are drawn from participation in several discussions with activists in unions, women's organizations and community groups in Toronto who are involved in struggles around the creation and mandate of the OTAB.

45. See, for example several presentations by Advocates for Community Based Training for Women (Toronto); David Robertson, "Technology, Skill and the Economy: A Response to David Wolfe and Leon Muszynski," xerox, not dated. The Steelworkers' Union in Canada has attempted to develop a position which encompasses the interests of their members in the devastated North American steel industry and those of workers in Third World countries. See United Steelworkers of America, "Empowering Workers in the Global Economy. A Labour Agenda for the 1990s," discussion paper prepared for Steelworkers' Forum, Royal York Hotel, Toronto, October 22–23, 1991.

46. Marcy Cohen, who represents women on the Canadian Labour Force

Development Board, is researching these shifts.

47. Aglietta, *A Theory of Capitalist Regulation*; Lipietz, Mirages and Miracles.

48. See "The Stateless Corporation," cover story of *Business Week* 14 May, 1990, pp. 98–106; "Going Global a Risky but Essential Move," *The Financial Post*, 4 December, 1989, p. 13.

Chapter Eight

Restructuring Work
New Work And New Workers In Post-Industrial Production

Catherine Casey
University of Auckland

Preface

This paper discusses the structural changes, and their implications, that are occurring in the world of work. To preface the paper a few words explaining why studying work is important to the study and practice of education would seem to be in order.

Analysts of education have spent several decades trying to understand the relationships between schooling and social reproduction. Various commentators have been interested in the potential of education to provide greater numbers of trained employees, especially technologists, scientists and managers who would enable the growth of advanced capitalist economies. Education, according to this functionalist viewpoint, was supposed to meet the needs of an expanding industrial economy and its social system. More recently, this same tradition has focused renewed attention on the ways the schooling system has adopted the values and practices of the corporate business world, promoting the latter's modernizing and 'reforming' influence in the organization of schooling.

Other commentators, particularly the 'new' sociologists of education, while wishing to reject the functionalist framework, did not quite make the paradigmatic shift they aspired to. But that is not our concern here. What they did do in their excavations of the mechanisms of social reproduction of inequalities and the ideological construction of legitimate knowledge was to introduce a critical focus on the role of class, gender and race in patterns of structural inequality and disadvantage. The 'new' sociology of education talked about reproduction and resistance and believed in social transformation through transformed practices of schooling.

As we now know, by the 1980s the rhetoric of reproduction and resistance had run its course and little observable social transformation had occurred. There was a subsequent move to other sites of analysis, particularly in North America, of popular culture as the new site for resistance and change. At the same time, the broader tradition of critical social theory that was informing much of the new sociology of education was struggling with its own crisis in historical materialism, and was retreating from 'old-fashioned' Marxist productionism including, of course, the old labour social movements, and focusing on culture — discourse, subjectivity, knowledge. And, simply put, post-structuralism emerged. Classical Marxism's concepts of ideology and class-based power structures were abandoned in the wave of disbelief in the fading narratives of modernity.

While, again, the intricacies of that story are not our concern here, what is important for us now is that this academic heritage has moved away from the 'old' struggles of the left and the sites around which it once organized. Work, like workers, has been given up on. The working class, Marcuse announced, is now politically integrated, and attention has subsequently shifted to the new social movements: feminism, ecology, identity, and so forth. Hence, with the demise of historical materialism, the rise of post-structuralism and the focus on the new social movements, few theorists, either educational or social, other than the unreconstructed Marxists, and of course business analysts, are particularly concerned with the world of work. Yet, work nonetheless remains a primary site of socialization and a formative condition of adult life and social organization. We ignore it theoretically at our peril.

This paper is about the changes in the character and form of the institution of work in modern industrial society. It implicitly deals with the structure and experience of paid industrial work. It does not deal with the categories of unpaid work, nor the specificities of particular occupational or gendered experiences. The effort is to explore the phenomenon of industrial work in broad terms, and to make sense of the qualitative shifts now occurring in its form and meaning. The risk in taking a general view is to render invisible the particular experiences of minority and gendered groups — typically women's work that is often treated separately. But working-class women have always participated in industrial work, and increasingly in post-industrial work, as much as men have (however unequally rewarded). The following essay implicitly recognizes and honours that participation.

Introduction

This paper explores the changes in work that have occurred in advanced industrial capitalist societies in the decades since the Second World War. Specifically, these changes are those brought about by the introduction of automated machine technology and electronic communication and information technologies in the workplace and in the cultural sphere of social life more broadly. These developments are manifestations of a qualitative shift that is occurring in society that is both a manifestation of, and creating, a 'post-industrial society.' The paper will describe the character of the 'new work' and discuss its impact upon the worker in the emergent post-industrial conditions. Following a brief review of the arguments in the 'new technology' debate the paper will discuss the actual changes in work that are being brought about by the expansion of automation technology and new information technologies in the workplace.

The New Technology Debate

Since the 1940s and '50s social analysts, industrialists and labour unionists, have been aware of the growing impact of new technology, (e.g. Marcuse, 1941; Giedion, 1948; Lumer, 1962; Walker, 1957; United Steelworkers of America, 1960) especially automation, on traditional industrial production. Coinciding with the advance of new technology into the workplace, analysts have also observed a shift from an economy based on the production of material goods to one increasingly centred around the provision of services, and of information, that has been occurring in advanced western industrial economies over the postwar decades (see especially Bell, 1973; Aronowitz, 1973, 1981; Harrison and Bluestone, 1988; Gorz, 1980, 1989; Reich, 1991).

This shift in the productive sphere has generated considerable commentary, and within the discourse, there are serious disagreements about the nature and impact of these changes. For some (Bell, 1973; Toffler, 1980), the problems generated by industrial capitalism are in the process of being solved by evolutionary transformations in technology and the economy. The shift from blue-collar, noisy, dirty and physically demanding work into cleaner, quieter and allegedly more complex and desirable white-collar work is resolving many of the problems associated with the organization of industrial work and the traditional sources of dissatisfaction and conflict.

Similarly, other post-industrial social analysts (Illich, 1972; Schumacher, 1974; Bahro, 1978) tended to greet the coming post-industrial era with an optimistic outlook. These earlier analysts of the 1960s and '70s argued for a low-tech, deindustrialized, 'small is beautiful' alternative to the corporate state. They saw in the new service economy and in automation possibilities for freedom from the drudgery, oppression and gradual deskilling of industrial work. They argued for the possibilities of decentralized, cooperative, non-bureaucratic and peaceful economic and social alternatives, and they emphasized the increasing educational opportunities and attainments of a growing majority of the population. They believed that, for those workers remaining in the corporate sector, white-collar jobs would become more interesting and rewarding as they correspondingly demanded more highly educated people to perform the tasks of 'knowledge work' of the new economy. Some theorists looked for the potential in post-industrial societies to liberate people from the need to work and for possibilities for 'post-capitalist' social and political systems, and postmodern social movements (Bahro, 1978; Frankel, 1987). In particular, Andre Gorz's 1980 book, bid 'farewell to the working class,' and celebrated the new era's departure from class and class-based politics. For these observers, 'freedom from work' was the utopian promise of the post-industrial era.

For others (Braverman, 1974; Silverman and Yanowitch, 1974; Gouldner, 1976; Aronowitz, 1981; Beniger, 1986) the changes in industrial production and the shift into post-industrial conditions are causing widespread social problems including a further deskilling of work, unemployment, a growing class of low-paid service workers and community dislocation as factory towns close down. In this view, automation is displacing millions of workers from factory and machine work, many of them into service work, or into unemployment. It is generating a new polarization in skill and occupation, and consequently in social life, and its so-called utopian promises are far from being realized. The enforced displacement from industrial work has not equated, for the workers concerned, with 'freedom' from the cultural need to work or with new forms of self-determination. Instead there is a cultural dislocation experienced at the intrapersonal level, and a decline, if not eventual destruction, of the quality of social life and cohesion.

Marx and Engels argued that the reductionism of capitalist economic rationality would have emancipatory potential, as the power relations between the classes it had established became obvious, and the proletariat assumed its historical dialectical role (Marx and Engels [1888], 1967). Instead, as the capitalist economic system developed, it increasingly required that its economic rationality prevail over all other forms of rationality, and human goals and interests. While the economic rationalization of labour did indeed occur under capitalist industrial conditions, the predictions of Marx and Engels of the inevitable proletarian reaction to that, did not. Instead, the success of economic rationality and its dominance over the cultural sphere has led to the emergence of social and political conditions completely unforeseen by Marx. The nature of the emerging bifurcation of society presents vast new problems not just specifically in the organization of work, but in the organization of society at all levels, that were not anticipated by the earlier analysts of automation technology and society.

Most obviously, the expansion of mechanization, and now increasingly automation, has produced a major shift in the nature and forms of work in society since the 1950s. A post-industrial capitalist economy no longer requires as much work, from as many workers, as industrial economies did. Increasingly, workers are being displaced by the introduction of new technology, some into the currently growing service sector, most into unemployment or casualized, short-term employment. The fin-de-siecle condition witnesses, amid other social upheavals, the emergence of a new form of class polarization. In a few decades, it is likely that most of those who remain in work (in the advanced industrialized countries) will be retained in relatively privileged echelons in highly specialized occupations for the corporations (see Gorz, 1989) or in service work. While there are differences in the patterns and impact of post-industrial changes in different economies — especially between the United States and Europe (Lash and Urry, 1988) and particularly with regard to unemployment (Harrison and Bluestone, 1988), the similarities in the effects of automation and the reorganization of work in post-industrializing societies are significant. A further elaboration of the post-industrial condition will continue below. For the moment, I will turn to a discussion of work in industrial society from whence we have come.

Industrial Work

Every form of work, including pre-industrial, involves technology, from rudimentary tools and technique to sophisticated abstract technologies and skills. The core of the industrial revolution was the vision of continuous motion and continuity in production. The realization of this vision took many decades. It required the development of technology and technique that greatly expanded upon and surpassed simple manual technology and human skill. Its achievement was epitomized by the

Henry Ford style of management and system of production (following Taylorism) in the manufacture of automobiles at the beginning of the 20th century.

Industrialization is evoked by three terms: the division of labour, specialization and mechanization (see Giedion, 1948; Hirschhorn, 1984). Like Smith and Durkheim, the early industrialists believed that productivity increases with the division of labour. The division of labour and the specialization of work tasks within the factory led to the development of specialized machines for performing particular functions of the production process. The first mechanical devises grew out of a simulation and extension of human action (the loom, the spinning jenny, the metal lathe). Gradually, the systematic linkage of specialized machines enabled the mechanization of the entire production process. Similarly, specialization of work tasks enabled large-scale production, and the elimination of customized craft work. The mass market was created. In the wider social sphere occupational specialization not only effected dramatic social changes in the way people worked, but in the ways they organized their lives and communities.

In the course of the societal shift from agricultural to industrial work the problem of time, and later of skill, emerged. Time-keeping was the first requirement of industrial work. No-longer was the rule of the seasons and of the weather the standard for measuring the working day. Industrial time-keeping demanded new disciplines of the everyday habits of the worker. The working day was structured around a required number of hours of work from each worker. In addition, the time factor generated a set of new skills, such as dexterity, economy of motion and speed, which became the new physical requirements of industrial workers, especially those on the assembly line. These skills, combined with endurance and disciplined compliance to the rhythms of the machine, began to displace physical strength as the primary requirement of industrial work.

The assembly line represented the drive toward mechanization and the development of continuous and controlled movement, of both mechanical parts and human labour. It became the hallmark of industrial technology. The assembly line manifests the fundamental principles of mechanization: standardization, continuity, constraint and the reduction of work to simple specialized labour — the core principles of industrial culture. Its smooth, continuous operation was reliant on the standardization and precision of parts, and the continuous action of the workers. The inflexibility of the mechanical assembly line imposed rigid constraints on the workers' physical and mental movements. The assembly line requires and achieves the subjugation of the human body to the power of the machine. It epitomizes the character of work in industrial society.

As the factories became more and more systematically organized, following the principles of Taylorism, and productivity increased, workers, who had become increasingly disciplined by the inexorable rhythms of the machines imposed upon them, became increasingly alienated from their labour and their products. The worker's labour became devoid of inherent interest or value, and she became a cog in the supermachine of the factory, doing repetitive actions for 8-10 hours a day for 40–50 years. The worker's psychological and physiological factors were rarely taken into account by the owners and managers of industrial plants and only to the extent that difficulties and pathologies affected the smooth operation of the industrial enterprize. Taylorism, or 'scientific management' completed the process of the 'workers as machine' from the turn of the century onward.

Alienation, Ambivalence And Degradation

Scientific management, however, was never a complete nor smoothly implemented process. Alongside the triumph of the machine and the rationalization of work was another important characteristic of modern industrial work. Often overlooked by the industrial and management theorists was the human subjective experience of work. Evidence of the alienating and destructive effects of modern industrial work, following Marx's early observations and predictions, has continued to be well-documented by social scientists in recent decades (see, for example, the Special Task Force Report on Work in America, 1973). Much is based on the personal accounts of workers. Workers and their unions have long recognized the alienating character of modern industrial work (e.g. Baran and Sweezy, 1966; Fraser, 1968; Turkel, 1972). Owners and managers of industrial enterprises and academic researchers have also recognized it and measured it in its more quantifiable form: as rates of absenteeism, wild-cat strikes, and workers disruption and sabotage of factory production or bureaucratic processes. By and large, worker alienation and its resultant 'industrial conflict' has been regarded as an inevitable, but manageable, problem of industrial work. The study of industrial relations is devoted to its mitigation and management.

In most western countries the right to work is regarded as a fundamental human right and unemployment is seen as a serious social problem. Yet work is very often perceived as unwanted and painful toil, to be avoided as much as possible. Studies show that people's attitudes to work are more complex and contradictory than the apparent disparaging attitudes would suggest (Williams, 1968; Fraser, 1969; Goldthorpe, 1971; Turkel, 1981). Clearly, while the need to work is a socially constructed need, it is nonetheless subjectively viewed as an objective reality that operates to shape and structure people's social lives, as much as sustain their material needs. People need to work for all sorts of reasons, and most derive some sort of satisfaction, and sometimes pleasure from it, even when work is repetitive or monotonous and lacks any intrinsic meaningfulness. Socialization into the habits and processes of industrial production has been so successful that a breach in that experience for workers is experienced as a cultural abrogation, and considerable personal and social problems result.

Despite the alienating condition of industrial work, that is widely recognized by workers, an important contradiction in the behaviour of workers is also evident. Economic recessions occur periodically in industrial economies and workers are commonly laid-off from their jobs, especially those in the manufacturing sector. Likewise, in the emerging new economy, workers are being displaced rapidly by the introduction of automation technology. Under both sets of conditions, the reaction of workers and their unions is to fight for the right to keep their jobs, to keep ailing manufacturing plants open (Mann, 1987) and to concede conditions won in better times

(Bensman and Lynch, 1987; Fantasia, 1988). The effort is to preserve as much as possible their ability to participate in the processes of alienated labour. Despite the generally visible experience of alienation from oneself and one's labour in the industrial workplace, the experience of alienation from the social and cultural practices of work, is viewed by workers as much worse. Even in conditions of high redundancy payouts, and unemployment benefits, workers overwhelmingly prefer to participate in the paid workforce. For those who remain in jobs in the new economy, increasing unemployment is used as a threat against workers.

While the deep cultural and social importance of work established in industrial society continues in post-industrial society, the actual experience of work and the workplace have undergone, and are continuing, a process of change as sophisticated automation technology has expanded in the workplace, and as accompanying structural changes in the organization of work have occurred. The early critics of industrial work, and of advanced industrial society were concerned with the impact of automated industrial technology on workers and the workplace, and the concomitant increase in control that management and technology seemed to exert over workers.

Critical social theorists including Gramsci and the Frankfurt School critical theorists wrote about the increasing degradation and one-dimensional nature of man and of work in modern society. They despaired of the possibility for human emancipation and creative endeavour under the conditions of a 'colonization of the life world' by a technocratic rationality that was ever further reifying the products of human labour over those who had produced them. Their anticipation of the conditions of the post-industrial era were echoed some years later by the critics of the emerging society including Baudrillard, Lasch and Aronowitz. Increasingly and appropriately, their focus on the transformations in work and social life has attempted to reflect on the meanings engendered by the shift in the economic base from the materiality of industrial 'hard' ware, to the production of symbolic materiality in this 'time of the sign.' This viewpoint is similarly developed in this paper.

From Industrial To Post-Industrial Work

In the industrial age, people invented machines to reproduce and extend the capacity of the human body as an instrument of work. Machines that are mute (although hardly silent), precise and repetitive are able to be controlled according to a rational set of principles in ways that human bodies cannot be. The productive capacity of the industrial mechanization era vastly extended society's ability to produce things. The limitations on production formerly imposed by the limitations of the human body had been surpassed. Alongside the diminishing role of the worker's body in the production process, industrial technology and its management system also brought about a diminishment in the value of the worker. The reduction in the amount of physical and mental skill required from workers as the productive process was mechanized and centrally controlled, enabled the rationalization and bureaucratization of knowledge to become the basis of control.

The control of the productive activity was forcibly wrested from the hands of the workers, as the old 'artisan' and 'craftsman' skills became redundant. As Taylor envisaged, conception was increasingly divorced from execution. The removal of the 'brain work' from the execution of the tasks, rendered the simple labour of the worker more readily expendable. The perceived expendability of the worker in the scientifically managed factory became a useful rhetorical strategy that was employed against workers attempting to organize in opposition to the fragmentation of their work and the restructuring of their workplaces.

Following World War II there were signs that a major change in the direction of industrial technology had begun. The rapid development and expansion of electronic technology had made possible the development of a highly automated continuous-process technology. Among its earliest implications was the reversal of the typical trend of industrial society, foreseen by Marx and Durkheim, toward an increasing division of labour and specialization of function. This was first apparent in the change in the place of the worker's piecemeal labour as simply a unit in the production process. The simplest, most reductionist of worker's mechanical labour was immediately displaced by the automation of those tasks. The place of the worker in the overall process was changing. For those workers still required in an automated plant, there began a process of 're-skilling and 'up-skilling.' In highly automated workplaces the worker was no longer restricted to one highly specialized, routine task, and he was no longer tied to the rhythm of the machine. Increasingly, the worker was to be responsible for the overall operation of a complex unit of production.

Another significant change accompanied the decline in specialization. The fundamental requirements of industrial work, bodily exertion and manual dexterity, were being displaced by the requirements for rapid perception, attentiveness and the ability to analyze problems and make decisions. The rudiments of work had shifted from physical effort to the manipulation of electronic symbols through keyboards and press buttons (Gorz, 1989; Hirschhorn, 1984; Zuboff, 1989).

A further effect of the automation transformation of work that Gallie (1978) observed was the place of labour costs in the production equation. In his cross-cultural study of French and British oil refineries that were undergoing extensive automation in the 1960s and '70s, Gallie noted that the cost of labour was dramatically reduced in proportion to the costs of introducing the highly expensive automated production technology. Labour costs were also reduced in real terms as the requirement for manual labour declined and workers were laid off. At the same time, labour costs became a much more stable component of total costs, a fixed rather than a variable cost (Gallie, 1978: 8-9). Furthermore, continuous-process technology needed to be continually staffed irrespective of the level of production. Management, therefore, could no longer offset temporary recessions in the market by laying off labour. Consequently, in contrast to traditional mass-production industry, the new technical workers achieved a much higher level of job security.

This elevation of technical workers into a position akin to career status previously reserved for white-collar workers, because of their new highly demanded skills and job security, has also been examined by Gorz (1980; 1989), Gouldner (1976; 1979) and Aronowitz (1973; 1981) as evidence of the growing polarization and technicization of skilled workers. Nonetheless, the issues of control, management and integration of the workers and the work process remained contentious.

Aronowitz (1981) addresses the implications of polarization and restructuring of the traditional class bases of work. He points to the dramatic rise of the professional middle class in the 1970s and 1980s. For Aronowitz, the introduction of automation technology into the workplace is increasing the proportion of skilled to unskilled workers and simultaneously "resulting in the degradation of skill as such" (Aronowitz, 1981: 83). The new skills are not those which have traditionally been associated with the skilled workers of trade unions and socialist movements, and they correspond with the traditionally non-unionized, professional middle class. The new 'technical intelligentsia' has shown 'little propensity to conduct struggles about class formation.' He argues, that in the United States at least, the new manual workers within industries that have adopted advanced automation technology — oil, chemical, electronics — are relatively highly paid, and separated from the traditional skills of prior generations. They, in turn, have become depoliticized because of the decline of labour traditions and the industrial migration to small town, historically non-union areas south of the border into Mexico and beyond.

Aronowitz argues that the 'third industrial revolution' now underway in advanced economies, implies a 'transformation of the nature of the labour process' and also of the 'character of labour.' Following Marx's labour theory of value in which value is measured by quantities of labour time necessary for the production of commodities, Aronowitz argues that under the new technological changes, production becomes "more and more based upon technocratically-controlled systems of knowledge organization, rather than the control of labour" (Aronowitz, 1981: 86). This does not mean that labour has disappeared as a central aspect of production, or that its 'metaphoric/symbolic significance as the key to production is no longer present.' It remains the significant measure of value in abstract, and the 'regulative principle' of most of the world's production. However, the "quantity of labour required for production can no longer be evaluated in terms of time frames, since *knowledge* has become the main productive force" (Aronowitz, 1981: 83).

Alongside the emerging new 'knowledge work' has been the emergence of a vastly expanded service sector. The management processes of industrialized manufacturing generated the rise of a service class of white collar office workers, from clerical to management, and a sector of scientists and technical workers. The history and character of the service class has been well documented over the decades (Abercrombie and Urry, 1983; Giddens and Mackenzie, 1982; Gershuny, 1978; Kanter, 1975; Touraine, 1974; for examples). But in more recent years, the 'old' service class has itself undergone post-industrial transformations, in both composition and in work tasks. Importantly, a growing new division in the service sector has emerged. Many of the middle management workers comprising a large sector of the service class are no longer required by automated offices and there are accordingly fewer manual workers to supervise. Instead, the service class is growing at the lower-paid end, in particularly, the sector of fast-food workers and related service workers. Furthermore, in keeping with the post-industrial trend of a halting of increased specialization of function, these new service workers, although low-paid and quickly trained, are required to perform a wide range of responsibilities in dealing with customers and operating according to a company masterplan of standardized procedures and principles.

Post-Industrial Work

There is now virtually a consensus among contemporary analysts in both the U.S. and Europe that work in advanced industrialized societies has changed in qualitative ways, whether it is performed in automated material production sites, or in the service and information industries — the latter itself a new historical condition. In summary, my analysis of post-industrial work defines broadly two levels: the first level contains the more readily observable and quantifiable changes, being the introduction of automation technologies to the process of industrial production of material goods; the subsequent displacement of workers; the restructuring of work; and the reorganization of the workplace. The second level refers to the changes brought about by advanced technology, in the nature of production, and in what is being produced and valued. These changes include the primacy of knowledge and information as the new commodities, and the simultaneous 'informating' transformation of the workplace, in which the processes of the new technology also produce information. Furthermore, the new labour required of workers involves their minds more than their bodies, and computer technology enables new forms of surveillance and control over workers' activities to be built-in to the production process itself. There is a consequential collapse of old boundaries of work tasks; the appearance, at least, of a reversal of specialization and the division of labour characteristic of industrial work; and there is an altered hierarchy of supervision and control. The following section elaborates this analysis.

As automation technology takes over the work tasks previously performed by workers, millions of workers are being displaced from their jobs. One extensive empirical study in the U.S. by Leontief and Duchin (1986) shows that the "intensive use of automation will make it possible to achieve over the next 20 years significant economies in labour...." They go on to claim that, "Over 11 million fewer workers are required in 1990, and over 20 million fewer (will be required) in 2000 ..." (Leontief, 1986: 12). They predict that there will be a progressive increase in the proportion of professionals and a steep decline in the number and proportion of clerical workers. The increased demand for professionals is mainly for computer specialists and engineers (Ibid: 15). In the old, hard core heavy industries of steel and fero-alloys, there will be a further increase in their decline, not just because of robots displacing workers, but because of the rise of computer-controlled machine tools that require less heavy metals in their manufacture and use.

Over time, automation, work redesign, and organizational change enable fewer workers to produce more. One study in the electronics industry in the U.S. (Alic and Harris, 1988) shows that in the manufacture of televisions from 1971–1981 production output nearly doubled, from 5.4 million sets to 10.5 million. At the same time, jobs for production workers dropped by half over the same period (Alic and Harris, 1988: 670). Productivity on a unit output basis grew dramatically over the decade. During the same decade, U.S. industries moved many of their manufacturing operations to low-wage developing countries. It is estimated by the U.S. Department of Labor that more jobs were created in those offshore plants than were employed in domestic television manufacture. Similarly, in other industries, it is estimated that American manufacturing companies have carried out 90 per cent of all assembly work overseas.

The outcome of this process is a mixture of what some have called 'deindustrialization' (Bluestone and Harrison, 1982) domestically, in that the industrial productive work was moved offshore, and of 'post-industrialization' characterized by increased automation, centralized control of the information process, that is, productivity, stock, markets and so forth; and the dispersion and de-collectivizing of the workers.

The situation in Europe especially regarding growing unemployment is arguably even more visible and acute. In Germany, for example, unions and big companies negotiate over delaying the introduction of increasingly sophisticated new technologies into workplaces that are already highly automated (see Gorz, 1989; Lash and Urry, 1987). The disputes have become over the timing of the introduction of further advanced technology, not over the issue of its introduction per se — the latter issue is regarded as no longer realistically debatable. Rather, it is hoped that delaying further new technology introduction and its carefully managed timing will enable the ensuing social disruption to be somewhat lessened, and the potential for political instability averted.

I suggest that the deindustrialization (or displacement of industry) occurring within the U.S. (and in other advanced industrial countries) at the same time as the 'developing' countries are struggling to industrialize, is a relatively short-lived period in the overall shift occurring toward a post-industrial society. It is part of the qualitative shift in the sphere of production. It ensures that the traditional production of consumer goods is acquired at the cheapest possible source, while the 'information production' part of an enterprise's overall operation remains centralized. The labour process is increasingly decentralized and dispersed.

For the workers remaining in productive enterprizes, the experience and structures of their work are simultaneously changing with the restructuring generated, and enabled, by the introduction of automation and the concurrent production of more and new information. Mechanized industrial work was divided up into its smallest parts, and organized by linear hierarchies of supervision and control. In the new automated workplace, computer-linked 'multi-activity' jobs combine the tasks previously carried out by workers with different skills, and even occupational designations. In the office, for example, multi-activity teams, whose members all possess keyboard computer skills, carry out the tasks previously performed by clerks, secretaries and lower-level administrative workers. Much of the unskilled, rote clerical work is being eliminated (See examples in Drygulski and Wright, 1987; Gallic, 1978; Zuboff, 1988). In corporate industrial organizations even senior managers, engineers, financial analysts and others create their own documents and increasingly prefer to communicate electronically with each other and their 'interfaces' (customers).

Many workplaces are being reorganized into open plan offices or networks of cubicled workstations, in which more traditionally observable status and job differentiation are reduced. The multi-activity teams operate with much higher degrees of flexibility and adaptability. In white-collar work, the workers are increasingly more 'professional' and highly-trained than in the past. Zuboff's (1988) study showed that the material alterations in the workers' means of production "were manifested in transformations at intimate levels of experience — assumptions about knowledge and power, their beliefs about work and the meaning they derived from it, the content and rhythm of their social exchanges, and the ordinary mental and physical disciplines to which they accommodated their daily lives" (Zuboff, 1988: pxiii). Following Blauner, who in 1964 had claimed that automation enables the worker to gain a sense of control over the work process and that it makes work more meaningful, interesting and involving than assembly line production, Zuboff argues that these changes gave workers new opportunities for self-realization through work. Other studies (Casey, 1993) are finding that the new workplace culture and the re-structuring of the means of production are experienced by workers, and management, in more complex, contradictory and unexpected ways.

The debate about the changes and the positive and negative effects of computer technology are extensive and on-going. A central element in the debate is the question of skill. On the one hand, the argument runs as follows: In industrial society, the assembly line semi-skilled worker is tied to his tasks, but his mind is free to wander. His private self is alienated from his labour, that does not require his full mental attention. In post-industrial conditions, the prototypical control-room operator is required to bring her own awareness to consciousness by co-ordinating and controlling both her own selective attention processes and behaviours, and the activities of the plant. The operator is required to be multi-skilled, aware and flexible. She must be able to understand the entire production process, so that she is ready to respond to unpredictable situations. "The post-industrial worker ... performs developmental tasks, operating at the boundary between old technical realities and the emergent ones" (Hirschhorn, 1984: 79). The worker's ability to learn and adapt becomes more important than his past training. A worker's tacit understanding of a particular machine is more important than his general education and knowledge. He retains a substantive self-concept as an agent in work. In this process, he experiences himself as 'one who adapts' (Hirschhorn, 1984).

This optimistic view of automation technology assumes that the new technology will provide workers with opportunities in which they can exercise new forms of skill and knowledge, especially to exercise critical judgement in managing the new machines. As work becomes more abstract, requiring flexibility and manipulability, workers experience new challenges and forms of mastery. In the workplace, the technological transformation engenders new approaches to organizational behaviour, one "in which relationships are more intricate, collaborative and bound by mutual responsibilities of colleagues" (Zuboff, 1988: 6). The integration of new technology across time and space allows managers and workers to overcome the constraints of their narrow functional perspectives and create new roles that are better suited to a 'data-rich' environment. As the range and quality of skills at each organizational level become similar, hierarchical distinctions become blurred. Authority becomes based upon appropriate 'fit' between knowledge and responsibility rather than upon ranking rules of traditional organizational structures. The new flows of information between multiple users create opportunities for innovative methods of information sharing and exchange. Such methods, it is argued, produce a deepened sense of collective responsibility and ownership.

This view also believes that automation will lead to a high degree of social integration. The work conditions associated with more traditional technologies and industrial relations have been definitively altered by the introduction of automation technology. This has led to a reduction in the level of industrial conflict and to closer relations between management and the workforce. Consequently, the integration of the workers into the existing social structure of advanced capitalist society is achieved.

Disturbing this rosy picture, is a counter view from a perspective that focuses more immediately on the worker's lived experience, and on the persistence of social relations tied to ownership and control. In industrial society, workers' organizations traditionally demanded the right to have some say in what goes on in the workplace, and in what workers are required to do. The tradition of workers' organization, while rapidly eroding in this new era (Aronowitz, 1981; Gorz, 1989; Heckscher, 1988; Feldman and Betzold, 1990), retains a perspective that is less concerned with managing the new technology than it is concerned with its impact upon jobs, and work conditions, and upon the person of the worker. Some of the critics, probably more visibly so in Europe (Gorz, 1989 cites German examples in particular; Negt, 1984; Kern and Schumann, 1984), recognize that the new computer technology fundamentally reorganizes the infrastructure of the material world and, not just although most immediately, of the workplace. Critics argue that the human capacity for critical judgment is given over to the new intelligent machines, and workers become ever more docile and dependent. This situation causes workers to become more cynical and distanced from one another as their jobs become more routinized and perfunctory. They look for more ways to escape their jobs, and conflicts in the workplace increase. Social alienation and disaffection exacerbates already serious social and political decline and the resurgence of sectarian political influence.

Furthermore, the new technology simultaneously employs surveillance techniques to watch workers' every activity, and to ensure their conformity to the company. The ability to manage by remote control, circumvents the traditional face-to-face encounter, and the negotiating process with workers. Technology displaces interpersonal contacts, and it becomes a new site of tension and sublimated confrontation. Information technology not only extends the process of mechanized technology to displace human agency, it also accomplishes the simultaneous production of information. For example, the computer systems that make it possible to automate office work also create the means to gain a vast overview of an organization's operations. Many levels of data are able to be coordinated and accessed for a variety of analytical purposes, including the ability to finely measure and predict production rates and performance to the monitoring of every keystroke. In other words, information technology not only produces action, it also produces a language that makes visible and knowable many more elements, material and symbolic, of the production process. In this latter respect, information technology fundamentally differs from mechanized technology. It produces information, symbols and signs simultaneously with the production of objects.

Discussion: Implications Of The New Work

The story of the transition from industrial work to post-industrial work raises important new questions about work, education, knowledge and society. Despite the considerable and accelerating changes in work, the world of work remains a site of primary socialization of individuals, and a primary site of social organization. One's relation to work — whether in or out of it — continues to shape one's life experiences and chances. The socially constructed meanings of work in industrial society have not yet diminished as industrialism fades. The continuing impact of work on the way society is organized, and on the formation of the individual person, remains effective in this transitional, post-industrial moment. The question of how we will educate our young people for a future in which work is qualitatively different from that of their parents is, at the end of the day, the most important question facing educators in the 1990s.

In this new era workers are told that the new high-tech productive work, and its new products, knowledge and information, no longer require their old industrial skills, and the habits of those old routines and processes. The new era demands from workers 'skills' they have not been socialized to have — flexibility, adaptability, a familiarity with symbols and not with matter and, above all, a willingness to 'be on duty' to 'attend' to the smart machines now possessing the disembodied knowledge and control of the production process. Clearly, a great deal of learning already goes on at work through the processes of both a manifest and a hidden curriculum. The implications of these learning processes for the formation of the person need to be more fully explored in future research.

We do not know yet the full implications of the qualitative transformations occurring in both the productive and cultural spheres of society. It appears from this vantage that in the coming decades a highly technological society will emerge in which some people work a great deal and many others work very little or not at all. Such a possible condition necessarily has determinative implications for the way in which society will be organized, a question beyond the focus of this paper. Nonetheless, as social analysts or educators it is our task to look for seeds and practices of new forms of social life and to develop new educational practices that will enable the construction of a social world beyond the 'iron cage' (Weber [1905], 1958) of industrialism.

References

Abercrombie, N. and Urry, J., *Capital, Labour and the Middle Classes*. London: Allen and Unwin, 1983.

Alic, John A. and Harris, Martha Caldwell, "Employment Lessons from the US Electronics Industry," in Pahl, R. E. (ed.), *On Work*. U.K: Basil Blackwell, 1988.

Aronowitz, Stanley, *False Promises: The Shaping of the American Working Class*. New York: McGraw Hill, 1973.

_____, *The Crisis in Historical Materialism*. Massachusetts: Bergin and Garvey, 1981.

Bahro, Rudolf, *The Alternative*. London: New Left Books, 1978.

_____, *From Red to Green*. U.K.: Verso, 1984.

Baran, Paul and Sweezy, *Monopoly Capitalism*. U.K.: Hamondsworth, 1966.

Bell, Daniel, *The Coming of Post-industrial Society*. U.K.: Harmondsworth, 1973.

Beniger, James R., *The Control Revolution*. Cambridge, Mass.: Harvard University Press, 1986.

Bensman, David and Lynch, Roberta, *Rusted Dreams: Hard Times in a Steel Community*. Los Angeles: University of California Press, 1987.

Bluestone, Barry and Harrison, Bennett, *The Deindustrialization of America*. New York: Basic Books, 1982.

Braverman, Harry, *Labor and Monopoly Capital*. New York: Monthly Review Press, 1974.

Fantasia, Rick, *Cultures of Solidarity: Consciousness, Action and Contemporary American Workers*. Los Angeles: University of California Press, 1988.

Feldman, Richard and Betzold, Michael (eds.), *End of the Line: Autoworkers and the American Dream*. Urbana and Chicago, Ill.: University of Illinois Press, Urbana and Chicago, 1990.

Frankel, Boris, *The Post-industrial Utopians*. Madison,Wis.: University of Wisconsin Press, 1987.

Fraser, Ronald (ed.), *Work: Twenty Personal Accounts*. London: Penguin Books, 1968.

Gallie, Duncan, *In Search of the New Working Class*. Cambridge, U.K.: Cambridge University Press, 1978.

Gershuny, Jonathon, *After Industrial Society?* New Jersey: Humanities Press, 1978.

Giddens, A., and Mackenzie (eds.), *Social Class and the Divisions of Labour*. Cambridge, U.K.: Cambridge University Press, 1982.

Giedion, Sigfried, Mechanization takes Command. New York: W. W. Norton, 1948.

Goldthorpe, J. H., *The Affluent Worker: Industrial Attitudes and Behaviour*. Cambridge, U.K.: Cambridge University Press, 1968.

Gorz, Andre, *Farewell to the Working Class* (trans. Michael Sonenscher). Boston: South End Press, 1982.

_____, *Critique of Economic Reason* (trans. Gillian Handyside & Chris Turner). London and New York: Verso, 1989.

Gouldner, Alvin, *The Dialectic of Ideology and Technology*. New York: Oxford University Press, 1976.

Harrison, Bennett, and Bluestone, Barry, *The Great U-Turn: Corporate Restructuring and the Polarizing of America*. New York: Basic Books, 1988.

Heckscher, Charles, *The New Unionism: Employee Involvement in the Changing Corporation*. New York: Basic Books, 1988.

Hirschhorn, Larry, *Beyond Mechanization: Work and Technology in a Postindustrial Age*. Cambridge, Mass.: MIT Press, 1984.

Illich, Ivan, *Tools for Conviviality*. London: Fontana, 1975.

Kanter, Rosabeth Moss, *Men and Women of the Corporation*. New York: Basic Books, 1977.

Lash, Scott and Urry, John, *The End of Organized Capitalism*, Madison, Wis.: University of Wisconsin Press, 1987.

Leontief, Wassily and Duchin, Faye, *The Future Impact of Automation on Workers*. London: Oxford University Press, 1986.

Lumer, Hyman, *Is Full Employment Possible?* New York: New Century Publishers, 1962.

Mann, Eric, *Taking on General Motors*. Los Angeles: University of California Press, 1987.

Marcuse, Herbert, *One-Dimensional Man*. New York: Abacus, 1964.

Marx, K. and Engels, F., *The Communist Manifesto* (1888). A. J. P. Taylor (ed.), London: Penguin, 1968.

Pahl, R. E. (ed.), *On Work: Historical, Comparative and Theoretical Approaches*. U.K.: Basil Blackwell, 1988.

Reich, Robert, *The Work of Nations: Preparing Ourselves for 21st Century Capitalism*. New York: Alfred Knopf, 1991.

Schumacher, E. F., *Small is Beautiful*. London: Abacus, 1974.

Silverman, Bertram and Yanowitch, Murray (eds.), *The Worker in Postindustrial Capitalism: Liberal and Radical Responses*. New York: Free Press, 1974.

Smith, Adam, *The Wealth of Nations* (1776). U.S.: Penguin Books.

Taylor, Frederick, *The Principles of Scientific Management* (1911). New York: W. W. Norton, 1967.

Toffler, Alvin, *The Third Wave*. London: Pan Books, 1980.

Turkel, Studs, *Working*. New York: Avon Books, 1974.

Touraine, Alain, *The Post-industrial Society*. New York: Random House, 1971.

Upjohn Institute for Employment Research, *Work in America*. Report of a Special Task Force to the Secretary of Health, Education and Welfare, Cambridge, Mass.: MIT Press, 1973.

United Steelworkers of America, *An Experiment in Education* (No.PR-108). Pittsburgh, Penn.: United Steelworkers of America, 1960.

Walker, Charles, *Toward the Automated Factory*. New Haven, Conn.: Yale University Press, 1957.

Weber, Max, The Protestant Ethic and the Spirit of Capitalism (1905). New York: Charles Scribner Sons, 1958.

Williams, Raymond, "The Meanings of Work," in Fraser (ed.), 1968.

Wright, Barbara Drygulski (ed.), *Women, Work, and Technology*. Ann Arbor, Mich.: Michigan Press, 1987.

Zuboff, Shoshana, *In the Age of the Smart Machine: The Future of Work and Power*. New York: Basic Books, 1988.

Chapter Nine

Rethinking Vocational Learning

Nancy S. Jackson
McGill University

The system of vocational learning in North America is profoundly anachronistic. In an era of widespread intellectual renewal and restructuring of knowledge, from post-positivism and postmodernism to post-Fordism and post-Keynesianism, vocationalism sits like a fossil, trapped in a bedrock of empiricism and behaviourism. Indeed, in recent years these characteristics have being elevated to new heights, in the name of learning that is efficient, accountable and relevant to industry. In the name of renewal, we have retrenchment.

This paper is concerned with the theoretical foundations for a different kind of renewal in vocational learning. It is preliminary and exploratory; no practical pedagogical solutions will be offered here. This work is driven by the belief that the whole edifice of vocationalism cannot and will not be reformed by tinkering and adjustment from within. On the contrary, dozens of frustrated vocational educators have said to me over the last decade that standing within the system, it is nearly impossible to see what's wrong with it. Its logic is common sense and persuasive; its administrative processes are compelling; it feels monolithic and hegemonic. Who can be against it and where would you start?

In this paper I have chosen to start with some questions about the nature of work itself, and how it has been conceptualized for educational purposes. When I talk about work throughout this paper I have in mind what might be called 'labour,' that is non-professional work, the kind of work where people might say popularly that they get paid for what they 'do' rather than what they 'know.' In fact, it is exactly with this distinction that I want to begin.

Much has been written in the last decade about both the restructuring of work and the restructuring of knowledge. For the most part, these writings have remained bounded by quite separate discourses, the domain of labour process theory on the one hand and postmodernism on the other. Educators, with few exceptions, have watched these theoretical debates from the sidelines, whilst preparing teachers for Monday morning. For vocational educators in particular, such theoretical concerns about the nature of work or knowledge appear a far cry from the problems and pressures of keeping kids in school and helping them get ahead.

In this paper I want to try to narrow this gap between contemporary social theory and vocational practice. At the very least, I want to sketch the ground for such a project, exploring how conceptions of 'work' and 'knowledge' might be brought closer together. From their intersection I want to point toward a restructured vision of the 'vocational,' not only as a domain of educational action but as an important site of cultural transformation and political struggle.

In the first section of this paper, I will problematize the concept of 'working knowledge' as a point of departure for the remainder of the investigation. Next, I will examine briefly how vocational know-how has conventionally been represented in North America by the prevailing empiricism of scientific management. Then I will contrast this with a theoretical approach informed by activity theory, using clerical work as the case in point, and draw on some examples from my own research on clerical learning to illustrate the implications of such a shift. Finally I will comment on the significance of this analysis for the project of building a critical pedagogy for vocational learning.

From Work And Knowledge To Working Knowledge

I want to formulate a problematic here which is both epistemological and political. My objective is to investigate the nature of work in such a way that real individuals appear as its knowing and acting 'subjects,' This is not to wrest these 'subjects' from their social and historical circumstances in the workplace, to reconstitute them as individuated, psychologized subjectivities. On the contrary, what is needed is to discover them precisely as the subjects of the social relations of work, but with their subjectivities in tact.

The subject-status of workers is an important focus of analysis from both sociological and educational perspectives. In a sociological context, it is important to counter the tendency of labour process studies to represent individual activity in the workplace as if it simply emerged spontaneously out of organizational design. I will argue that neither the nature of work nor the character of individual action in work can be understood in this objectified and objectifying mode. Quite the contrary. Organizational design and indeed all activities of 'production' are themselves constituted in and through individual decision-making and action. So the question arises, what is the nature of individual action/activity in work through which workplaces come to function as they do? As educators, we need to understand these relations between work and its subject as a precondition to a dynamic and enabling vocational pedagogy.

In an academic era so obsessed with the status of the 'subject' in nearly every field of knowledge, it is interesting that the 'subjects' of work, or indeed of learning related to work, have received such limited attention in theoretical or epistemological terms. This is not an incidental or accidental feature of conventional wisdom or academic tradition. It is instead a product of the standpoint of those who do the theorizing. Labour is mostly problematized in our society from places which workers do not occupy, that is the position of those whose interest is in managing and controlling it. Thus, the conceptualizations of work which are ready at hand construct work in terms that objectify and abstract it, to serve the purposes of those whose need is to 'know' it in this form (e.g. as a cost item on a balance sheet). Similarly, ideas about learning for work in North America have almost always been constructed by academics, as a form of education intended for 'other people's children'. In this context it is not surprising that vocational programs look like they do.

While the dominant understandings of work and learning for work cannot ultimately be separated, historically or theoretically, in this paper I will restrict my focus strictly for pragmatic reasons to the latter, to how vocational educators have conceptualized work for the purposes of learning.

Learning For Work

There is a startling uniformity in how work as the object of vocational learning has been talked about for almost a hundred years. The basic conceptual framework is drawn from the prevailing social and industrial discourses of the turn of the century. The learning thought necessary to be imparted through schooling for the masses of young people were the skills of every day manual labour, in factories for the boys and in the home for the girls. The nature of these skills was said to be derivable through a judicious combination of systematic science and common-sense observation. In the words of Franklin Bobbitt, noted proponent of the scientific approach to curriculum:

> The central theory is simple. Human life, however varied, consists in the performance of specific activities. Education that prepares for life is one that prepares definitely and adequately for these specific activities. However numerous and diverse they may be for any social class, they can be discovered. This requires only that one go out into the world of affairs and discover the particulars of which these affairs consist. These will show the abilities, attitudes, habits, appreciations and forms of knowledge that men [sic] need. These will be the objectives of the curriculum. They will be numerous, definite and particularized. The curriculum will then be that series of experiences which children and youth must have by way of attaining those objectives (Bobbitt 1918: 42).

This basic, common sense, empiricist approach to defining the objects of schooling forms the bedrock of the vocational tradition in North America. In fact, the educational reform documents of the 1980s use language that is startlingly similar to that of Bobbitt in 1918. Over the intervening years, this general 'scientific' approach has been elaborated into various systems for curriculum design and delivery, most of which share a basic commitment to detailed empirical specification of objectives and insistence on a behavioural approach to instruction and assessment. In this mode, the learning process is broken down into 'performance objectives' which are seen to be objective and measurable, even democratic, since everyone can agree about what is being achieved. Emphasis on 'knowledge components' is seen as a barrier to effective learning and is systematically suppressed in the instructional framework. This approach to learning is often recommended on the grounds that it closely approximates the working environment, a 'real-job' approach to learning, and produces know how that is practically useful in institutional life. It is seen as the kind of learning that "prepares for life" equally well in 1990 as in 1910.

Admittedly, this is a rather cursory account of an otherwise diverse field of vocational instruction. But I will rely on the general familiarity of the reader with the kind of educational practices which would share these basic assumptions and thus fall broadly within this framework. I will take the liberty of using this broad sketch as a point of departure for a process of critical appraisal of what is routinely omitted from such approaches.

Knowing Without Knowers; Action Without Actors

My central concern here is with how the objects of vocational learning are understood. The conventional approach begins much as Bobbitt does, with a 'look and see' approach — treating knowledge and skills as naturally occurring phenomena, locatable empirically by examination of work processes in the world around us. In this mode, vocational knowledge and skills are constructed as stable objects which stand outside the learner, and can be discovered in the form of 'tasks' to be mastered. Such task and their mastery are seen to be unambiguously definable and accessible to evaluation in a systematic and unambiguous manner. This view of vocational know-how is enforced through existing forms of curriculum organization which insist on the use of performance indicators to render the instructional goals explicit and measurable.

This method of approaching the educational process involves the objectification of vocational learning. 'Performance' becomes a form of action from which the 'knowing subject' has been removed for all practical purposes. It is a moment of abstraction, a separation of subject and object, a rupture in the internal continuity of knowledge and action. It is this separation which provides the possibility of external definition and control — it inserts a point of authority outside the moments of teaching and learning from which these activities may be defined, measured, evaluated for someone else's purposes.

The imposition of this kind of separation on the goals of vocational learning satisfies the needs of administrators for a rational and accountable curriculum management process (see Jackson, 1993). But I will argue here that it has the effect of disorganizing vocational activity for the purposes of the individuals whose 'need' is to master it as a form of practical action.

Work As Practical Action

Some interesting theoretical resources for a radically different view of work processes and their representation for the purposes of learning are available in a growing area of scholarship known as activity theory. It is an international and interdisciplinary development, drawing heavily on the work of early 20th-century Russian social psychologists and critical language theorists (most notably Vygotsky, Leont'ev, and Luria). Contemporary work in activity theory is posing some interesting challenges to education by questioning the traditional assumptions of cognitive and developmental psychology on which much of educational theory has been based. I have found their work extremely interesting and suggestive, in ways that I hope to illustrate briefly here, though I do not mean to represent my own work in this area as an instance of activity theory per se.

Broadly speaking, activity theorists are concerned with the connection between the cognitive and the social domains and with the problem of learning in that context. The basic line of thinking derives from developments in critical linguistics at the turn of the century. That is, activity theory argues that the meaning of action, like the meaning of language, is never abstract or objectified, but always embedded in its surroundings. The basic premise is that human activity is part of a system of social relations and that "… if we remove human activity from the system of social relationships and social life, it would not exist" (Leont'ev, 1981:46–47). It calls for a concept of 'activity' which includes "goals, means, and constraints operating on the subject" (Cole, 1985: 151).

Applying these premises to the study of work, activity theory directs attention to the "process that active subjects use to form real connections with the world of objects" (Leont'ev in Cole, 1985: 151). Researchers have been using this approach for a decade to study the activities of both work and work learning in formal and informal settings (Lave and Wagner, 1991; Lave, 1988; Orr, 1988; Suchman, 1987; Sternberg and Wagner, 1986; de la Rocha, 1985; Scribner, 1984). They have observed that competent actors in any situation draw upon a range of clues provided by the environment and accumulated through experience over time, to address the 'task at hand.' This phenomenon has been called 'skilled practical thinking' (Scribner, 1984).

But theorists are careful to point out that drawing a relation between action and its environment is more than a matter of seeing actions in 'context.' Rather, an adequate conceptualization of 'skilled practical thinking' involves recognizing the inextricability of task from environment, or "incorporat[ing] the environment into the problem itself" (Scribner, 1984: 23).

For my purposes, the most interesting and well developed example of this kind of analysis applied to work processes is the detailed investigation done by Lucy Suchman (1983; 1987) of the nature of clerical labour. Working in the Palo Alto laboratories of the Xerox corporation, the immediate objective of her work is to explain the persistent difficulties encountered by systems analysts trying to automate clerical work processes.

According to Suchman, systems analysts routinely begin with the premise, based in management theory, that "... office work is essentially procedural in nature, involving the execution by office workers of a prescribed sequence of steps." In this view, a smooth, orderly work process is achieved by the "compliance of employees" in adequately carrying out the specific procedures. Suchman refers to this view of office work as the "procedural paradigm," and reports that it has associated with it certain "persistent troubles." These troubles are related to the "imprecise," "informal" or "unstructured" character of clerical activities compared to the "step-wise" instructions required for a successfully functioning computer program. Suchman (1983: 321) refers to this problem as the "stubbornly ambiguous properties of office procedures."

The crux of this problem, according to Suchman, lies with the "underlying theory about human organization and action" on which both management science and computer science rely. She rejects outrightly the view that a solution to programming problems can be found through more complete specification of office procedures. She argues instead that the whole model needs to be turned on its head. That is, according to Suchman, the "definite meaning" of office activities will be found, not in procedural specification of tasks, but in the organization of practical action itself. The orderliness which characterizes office work processes will be found to arise, not as a prior condition, but only as a "constituent feature of the work of getting them done" (1983: 321). Suchman uses the term "situated action" to underscore this view of the nature of work activity and to contrast with conventional practices of definition by abstraction. She writes:

> Every course of action depends in essential ways upon its material and social circumstances. Rather than attempting to abstract action away from its circumstances and represent it as a rational plan, the approach is to study how people use their circumstances to achieve intelligent action (1987: 50).

Looking at clerical work in this way, Suchman discovers that the "smooth flow" of office procedures is "an outcome to which practitioners orient their work — it is not the work itself." Smoothness is achieved as clerical workers make decisions about the "operational significance" of objects and events on a case by case basis, and the "social and material make-up of the office setting serve as [a] central resource" for their decision making. Significantly, as Suchman points out, this view "recommends an understanding of office work that attends to the judgmental practices embedded in the accomplishment of procedural tasks" (1983: 327).

If taken seriously, the implications of this transformation in the representation of clerical work are profound. If clerical workers are seen as the originators of order and routine, rather than as compliant with an order dictated by others, it would radically change the official view of their work: its complexity, its place in an organizational hierarchy, its relation to other jobs for the purposes of pay and career mobility. These may indeed be good reasons for resistance to the official adoption of such a view in departments of personnel administration, and good reason for advocates for pay equity to be interested.

In the face of such conflicting representations, the ineluctably political character of the educational process also comes clearly into view. How we teach a work process depends fundamentally on how we conceptualize it or, in Suchman's phrase, our "underlying theory" of the object of learning. The staunch empiricism of traditional vocational instruction systematically denies and obscures this theoretical and political moment, thus rendering the practice of vocational learning a highly ideological process.

Clerical Work In Action

Here I want to take a more empirical turn and try to show in ordinary language what clerical work might look like if our view was informed by such a radically different approach to the topic. I have been doing research on clerical work and learning intermittently for a number of years and have found it very useful to think about clerical settings in ways that share some features with the activity theory approach. Here I will draw on that research to give some very simple illustrations of clerical work activities reconceived. The example I will use is the common, everyday office activity of answering the phone.

Answering the telephone has long been talked about — and

taught in office programs — as a routine function that requires personal characteristics and skills such as having a pleasant voice, using a polite manner, writing accurate and legible messages, and knowing how to forward a call. Well, without even considering the formidable complexity of today's programmable phone systems, this picture of simplicity begins to disintegrate once we scratch the surface of this job. If we look more carefully, we can see that answering phone calls competently involves a variety of kinds of comprehension, problem solving and decision making that all depend upon local knowledge and individual judgment, whether or a small or large scale. For example, the problem of comprehension begins with the need to establish who is calling and who the calling party wants to speak with. Both of these determinations are essential in deciding what to do with the call, and either of them could be complicated. Lets take them one at a time.

Knowing 'who' is calling means more than being able to repeat, and perhaps spell, the name. It is tied up with a number of levels of judgment. For instance, the person answering the phone may need to decide whether the caller is a V.I.P., whether the call is of a business or personal nature, and whether it is of routine or an urgent nature. The caller could even be a 'crank,' a threatening client, or it could be a personal emergency. All of these situations would require vastly different responses from the competent office worker, and the problem of adequacy in responding to the call depends essentially on these matters of initial interpretation of its nature and significance. In familiar settings, all of these understandings are taken for granted, even by the person doing the work, until a problem arises.

Similarly, determining who the caller wants to speak with can be complicated in the extreme. It requires the person answering the phone to be generally familiar with the names and positions of employees of the organization, or familiar with the departments and the use of a directory in large firms. She needs to be able to determine whether the party requested does work for the firm, whether s/he is available, or failing that, when and how s/he can be reached. She needs to be able to take messages which will be coherent to the reader, and she needs to make judgments about how much information and of what kind to give to the caller about the activities of the person they are seeking. For example, she surely is expected not to say, "Ms. Jones told me to tell you she is not here right now." etc. If all attempts to match the caller with a desired party fail, she needs to be able to say with reasonable confidence that the caller has the wrong number or wrong information, etc. This may get her into another round of problem solving about how the caller can get correct information.

I once overheard a fascinating conversation illustrating this point when I was standing in the reception area of the Ontario Federation of Labour. The receptionist was obviously dealing with a caller who wanted to contact the Teamsters Union, which was not, at that time, an affiliate. Responding to this persistent and uninformed caller required the receptionist to have a basic knowledge of a very complex set of historical and political relationships in order to deal briefly and appropriately with the questions of the caller. I'm sure that busy receptionist had no idea with what keen interest and admiration I was eavesdropping on her conversation that afternoon!

In more routine ways as well, deciding how to respond to a caller depends on the type of calls which are expected in a given office setting and the range of circumstances which usually apply. I can best illustrate this with an anecdote from my research in an Office Administration program in a community college in the Toronto area. We interviewed students at several points in their program, including immediately upon their return from Work Week placements. The student I have in mind had just returned from spending a day at the reception desk in a small community organization. For her, learning to "do the phones" was a matter of figuring out why different people might be calling and what different kinds of action this organization had to offer. So, for example, aside from the business line, there was a crisis line, and she reported that she had realized part way through the day that answering this line required completely different strategies from the other calls. She said things like, "I eventually figured out that people calling in a crisis don't want to be put on hold and they don't want to hear canned music ..." and "... I had to learn to be calm over the phone," etc. So for this student, 'doing the phones' required learning to produce the appropriate forms of the relations between the organization and its clients. Nothing in her office procedures class had prepared her for these aspects of 'answering the phones.'

I could go on at some length analysing subsequent moments in the social relations of answering the phone. But the point of all this is that answering the phone is simply one moment in the work of organizing and processing the ongoing business of any given office environment. It cannot be competently performed without comprehending and participating in the production of meanings and priorities of this larger information process. No approach to job definition or training which emphasizes the behavioural aspects of the job can or will adequately represent the forms of practical action required to perform these functions competently in the lived situation. The significance of this analysis will be confirmed by anyone who has ever worked in an office environment where there was an incompetent receptionist and has seen the generalized dysfunction which ensues in such a circumstance.

In this context, the problem with a routine, procedural understanding of functions like answering the phone is not just 'narrowness' in a simple, linear sense, though this criticism certainly applies. But I have been arguing that the failure of this approach is actually much more complex and has to do with something we might call 'standpoint.' That is, the 'procedural' method of defining work objectifies the action in ways that rupture the essential relation of the worker to her or his own action on the job. It removes the worker as the knowing, thinking, sense-making subject of his or her own acts. She becomes not the creator or centre of action, but only its instrument. 'Performance' is conceptualized as the property of the employer and is defined not from the location of those who need to do it, but for the purposes of those who want to manage it and control.

These concerns take us to the heart of familiar debates about the politics of the workplace, but their relevance for education is conventionally overlooked.

Rethinking Vocational Learning

These examples suggest a very different method of conceptualizing vocational learning than the one inherited from Bobbitt. Instead of representing work activities as 'definite and particularized,' they make visible the unpredictable social processes in which behaviours like 'answering the phone' acquire their meaning for all practical purposes. In this approach, a 'task' is transformed from a static object into a dynamic relation between subject and object, in which the local meaning of the action is integral to its doing as well as to its learning.

A system of vocational learning that aimed to make these principles central would look very different from what we have today. It would necessarily attend to different aspects of work and recommend different priorities in learning. It would employ different methods of instruction and assessment, and promote a very different kind of understanding by the learner about the nature of work and his/her own place in it. It would produce a very different vision of 'what is to be learned' in the name of vocationalism. All of these solutions need to be the topic for another day.

At the very least, these preliminary investigations suggest that the problem of a critical pedagogy or liberatory practice of vocational learning has many dimensions. It will not be achieved the day that working people or their allies gain a stronger voice in the governing of our educational institutions, although this too is necessarily a part of a democratizing strategy. Its achievement is also tied to a struggle for control over the procedures that are used to 'define reality' at the heart of the vocational enterprise. In other words, we always need to ask how and by whom and in whose interests work is defined for the purposes of learning. From whose standpoint are work and learning described? Who is presented as the author of the action? Whose voice speaks with authority?

Contemporary vocational theorists who might take up this line of thinking have a lot of obstacles to overcome. But they would not be alone. There is a long tradition of voices calling for an understanding of work which puts the worker at the centre of the action and a version of work-learning in which the learner has dignity and power. Radical workers movements have championed such a cause for years, as Richard Johnson shows so eloquently in his study of 19th-century popular education movements (Johnson, 1979). In a more contemporary vein, workplace literacy and ESL campaigns are now widespread which aim to employ a truly learner-driven pedagogy and popular education approach. Even in the area of workplace skills training, traditionally the exclusive prerogative of employers, there are signs of the emergence of a labour-defined agenda including a commitment to learning which is worker-centred and developmental.

There is currently a plethora of skills training initiatives which are co-determined and have the potential to be arenas of political struggle. But none will make a difference unless the approach they take offers a radical transformation at the level the experience of the learner.

This returns me to my original proposition that the vocational enterprise needs to be restructured and reconceptualized from the inside out. It needs an alternative theoretical framework to provide the basis for large scale policy and institutional change that is not tied to the discourse of 'productivity and competitiveness.' And it needs a revitalized popular vision to bring an impetus for change that is driven from the ground up. In other words, we need nothing less than a 21st century movement for "really useful knowledge."

References

Bobbitt, J.F. (1918), *The Curriculum*. Boston: Houghton Mifflin.

Cole, M. (1985), "The zone of proximal development: where culture and cognition create each other," in J. Wertsch (ed.), *Culture, communication and cognition*. Cambridge: Cambridge University Press.

de la Rocha, O. (1985), "The reorganization of arithmetic practice in the kitchen," *Anthropology and Education Quarterly*, 16: 193–198.

Jackson, N. S.(1993), "If competence is the answer, what is the question?" *Australian and New Zealand Journal of Vocational Education Research*, 1, 1.

Johnson, R. (1979), "'Really useful knowledge': radical education and working-class culture, 1790–1848," in J. Clarke et al (eds.), *Working class culture*. London: Hutchison Publishers.

Lave, J. and E. Wenger (1991), *Situated learning: legitimate peripheral participation*. Cambridge: Cambridge University Press.

Lave, J. (1988), *Cognition in practice: Mind, mathematics and culture in everyday life*. Cambridge: Cambridge University Press.

Leont'ev, A.N. (1981), "The problem of activity in psychology," in J. V. Wertsch (ed.), *The concept of Activity in Soviet psychology*. Armonk, N.Y.: Sharpe.

Orr, J.E. (1988), "Transparency, representation, and embodied knowledge: Some examples from the diagnosis of machines," paper presented at the 87th Annual Meeting of the American Anthropological Association, Phoenix, AZ, November.

Scribner, S. (1984), "Studying working intelligence," in B. Rogoff and J. Lave (eds.), *Everyday cognition: Its development in social context*. Cambridge, Mass.: Harvard University Press.

Scribner, S. (1986), "Thinking in action: Some characteristics of practical thought," in R. J. Sternberg and R.K. Wagner (eds.), *Practical intelligence: Nature and origins of competence*. Cambridge: Cambridge University Press.

Suchman, L.A. (1987), *Plans and situated actions*. New York: Cambridge University Press.

Suchman, L.A. (1983), "Office procedure as practical action: Models of work and systems design," *ACM Transactions on Office Information Systems* 1, 4: 320–28.

Wertsch, J. (ed.) (1985), *Culture, communication and cognition: Vygotskian perspectives*. New York: Cambridge University Press.

Chapter Ten

Labour Unions, The Labour Movement, Working People
Resources For Ontario High School Teachers And Students

Jeffry Piker and Jim Turk

This list is intended to assist high school teachers and students in Ontario (and elsewhere) to find useful and interesting resources about unions, the labour movement, working people and related topics. It focuses on Canadian experiences but, like the labour movement itself, it also moves beyond Canadian boundaries. It contains references to books, magazines, A-V materials, lesson plans, places and people. It includes sources of information that are both general and specific, both contemporary and historical. Some materials will be found in high school libraries, departmental resource collections and school board resource centres; others will be found in libraries and resource centres in the community outside the school system. *This is just a start — for every item included here, there are many more excellent ones that are not listed. Add to it, yourself ...*

◆ = Highly Recommended as starting points

1) Books — Organized By General Topic

Social Studies

I. Abella and D. Millar, THE CANADIAN WORKER IN THE 20th CENTURY. Toronto: Oxford University Press, 1978 (overview of the role of working people in the life and times of Canadian society in this century).

S. Alinsky, RULES FOR RADICALS: A PRAGMATIC PRIMER FOR REALISTIC RADICALS. New York: Random House/Vintage, 1972 (a handbook "for those who want to change the world from what it is to what they believe it should be ...").

Bank Book Collective, AN ACCOUNT TO SETTLE: STORY OF THE UNITED BANK WORKERS. Vancouver: Press Gang Publishers, 1979 (clerks and tellers of the UBW tell why they decided to take on the banks, and what happened when they did).

H Braverman, LABOR AND MONOPOLY CAPITAL: THE DEGRADATION OF WORK IN THE 20th CENTURY. New York: Monthly Review Press, 1974 (the classic examination of the form and feeling of labour in the capitalist world — paperback).

N. Gough and G. Tickner, LANGUAGE AT WORK. Holt, Rinehart and Winston of Canada, 1987 (high school text focusing on effective communication; includes readings and exercises; see especially section on 'All in a day's work'; accompanied by Teacher Resource Book).

◆ B. Hamper, RIVETHEAD: TALES FROM THE ASSEMBLY LINE. New York: Warner, 1992 (autobiographical account of life on the GM assembly line).

C. Heron and R. Storey, eds., ON THE JOB: CONFRONTING THE LABOUR PROCESS IN CANADA. Kingston: McGill-Queen's University Press, 1986 (essays about Canadians on the job, highlighting important issues in the structure of work, the effects of workers' resistance, and the role of trade unions).

R. Laxer, ed., TECHNOLOGICAL CHANGE AND THE WORKFORCE. Toronto: OISE, 1978 (overview of tech. change in contemporary society, focusing on labour and management perspectives; 64 pp. paperback).

◆ C. Mackay, PAY CHEQUES AND PICKET LINES: ALL ABOUT UNIONS IN CANADA. Toronto: Kids Can Press, 1987 (an overview, designed specifically for schools, of labour history and union organization and operations; excellent graphics; in 'textbook' form, very accessible).

A. Mettrick, LAST IN LINE: ON THE ROAD AND OUT OF WORK — A DESPERATE JOURNEY WITH CANADA'S UNEMPLOYED. Toronto: Key Porter Books, 1985 (stories of jobless Canadians during the recession of the early '80s).

I. Munro et al, CANADIAN STUDIES: SELF AND SOCIETY. Toronto: Wiley Publishers, 1975 (Sections on 'Labour' and 'Capital and labour', within Chapter on 'The Canadian Economy').

S. Nemiroff, WORDS ON WORK: AN INTEGRATED APPROACH TO LANGUAGE AND WORK. Toronto: Globe/Modern Curriculum Press, 1981 (lesson ideas based on working people's comments about their work; see especially Unit on 'Managers and the managed').

◆ M. Novogrodsky and M. Wells, FRAMING OUR LIVES: PHOTOGRAPHS OF CANADIANS AT WORK. Toronto: Toronto Board of Education, 1989 (also includes a very useful teacher's guide).

J. Penny, HARD EARNED WAGES: WOMEN FIGHTING FOR BETTER WORK. Toronto: Women's Educational Press, 1983 (biographies of contemporary Canadian women fighting to better their lives in very difficult work environments).

J. W. Rinehart, THE TYRANNY OF WORK: ALIEN-

ATION AND THE LABOUR PROCESS. Don Mills, ON: Harcourt Brace Jovanovich, 1987, 2nd edition (examines the alienating nature of contemporary work and discusses alternatives).

C. Sylvester and M. Harris, ON STRIKE. Toronto: OISE, 1973 (issues relating to collective bargaining and strikes, based on Canadian labour disputes; 104 pp. paperback).

♦ S. Terkel, WORKING. New York City: Ballantine Books, 1985 ('People talk about what they do all day and how they feel about what they do').

♦ D. Wells, SOFT SELL: 'QUALITY OF WORKING LIFE' PROGRAMS AND THE PRODUCTIVITY RACE. Ottawa: Canadian Centre for Policy Alternatives, 1986 (a critical look at the promises and actual outcomes of QWL at Canadian workplaces, focusing on two contemporary case studies).

Technological Studies

♦ K. Braid, COVERING ROUGH GROUND. Vancouver: Polestar, 1991 (journeywoman carpenter and poet writes about her work).

♦ B. Hamper, RIVETHEAD: TALES FROM THE ASSEMBLY LINE. New York: Warner, 1992 (autobiographical account of life on the GM assembly line).

C. Heron et al, ALL THAT OUR HANDS HAVE DONE. Oakville. ON: Mosaic Press, 1981 ('A pictorial history of the Hamilton workers', including Sections on 'Life and Labour' and 'A Union Town').

W. Johnson, ed., WORKING IN CANADA. Montreal: Black Rose Books, 1975 (a collection of workers' experiences at a variety of jobs: auto plant, assembly line, printing shop, social agency, office, etc.).

J. Kuyek, THE PHONE BOOK: WORKING AT THE BELL. Kitchener, ON: Between the Lines, 1979 (an 'inside view' of employment experiences at Bell Canada workplaces).

M. Luxton, MORE THAN A LABOUR OF LOVE: THREE GENERATIONS OF WOMEN'S WORK IN THE HOME. Toronto: The Women's Press, 1980 (the work that women do that is never calculated as part of Canada's Gross National Product).

◆ M. Novogrodsky et al, FRAMING OUR LIVES: PHOTOGRAPHS OF CANADIANS AT WORK. Toronto: Toronto Board of Education, 1989 (also includes a very useful teacher's guide).

Unions: Structure And Activities

◆ C. Mackay, PAY CHEQUES AND PICKET LINES: ALL ABOUT UNIONS IN CANADA. Toronto: Kids Can Press, 1987 (an overview, designed specifically for schools, of labour history and union organization and operations; excellent graphics; in 'textbook' form, very easy to read).

NOTES ON UNIONS. Ottawa: Canadian Labour Congress, undated (seven fact sheets: Why Unions?, Labour History, How a Union Works, Labour's Structure, Labour's Social Objectives, Canadian Labour and the World, Glossary of Labour Terms).

ONTARIO FEDERATION OF LABOUR (OFL). Don Mills, ON: Education Department — has a variety of resource and curriculum materials about the organization and operation of unions (e.g. sample collective agreements, collective bargaining simulation exercises, policy statements on a variety of issues, etc.).

PEOPLE AND UNIONS: THE RIGHT COMBINATION. Don Mills, ON: Ontario Federation of Labour, 1986 (a 'Speaker's Guide to Union Education', to be used with the OFL/CLC video, 'Straight Facts'; out of print and out of data — suggestion: use C. Mackay, Pay Cheques and Picket Lines, instead).

History

◆ I. Abella, ed., ON STRIKE: SIX KEY LABOUR STRUGGLES IN CANADA — 1919–1949. Toronto: James Lorimer & Co., 1974 (accounts of six of the most important strikes in Canadian history: Winnipeg General Strike, Oshawa GM '37, Quebec asbestos '49 and others).

P. Bird, OF DUST AND TIME AND DREAMS AND AGONIES — A SHORT HISTORY OF CANADIAN PEOPLE. Toronto: The Canadian News Synthesis Project, 1975 (describes 'the experience of the ordinary and not so famous people who have made Canadian history'; paperback).

B. Broadfoot, TEN LOST YEARS: 1929–1939 — MEMORIES OF CANADIANS WHO SURVIVED THE DEPRESSION. Toronto: Paperjacks, 1975 (the memories of ordinary men and women about what the Depression was like).

J. Callwood, PORTRAIT OF CANADA. Toronto: Paperjacks, 1983 (a comprehensive, readable history of Canada which tells more about the lives and contributions of working people than is usually the case; Index contains many entries under 'Labour and labour movements', 'Unemployment', etc.).

M. Gross, ed., THE WORKINGMAN IN THE 19TH CENTURY. Toronto: Oxford University Press, 1974 (Sections on 'Work,' 'Working class life,' 'Organizing the working man,' etc.).

◆ C. Heron, THE CANADIAN LABOUR MOVEMENT. Toronto: James Lorimer and Co., 1989 (best recent short history of Canadian labour).

C. Lambie and P. Watson, THE CANADIAN WORKERS. Nelson Canadian Studies Series, undated (historical and social perspectives; 50 pp. paperback).

R. Laxer, ed., UNION ORGANIZATION AND STRIKES. Toronto: OISE, 1978 (stories of four important strikes in

Canadian history, 1910–1950; 103 pp. paperback).

D. Lewis, THE GOOD FIGHT: POLITICAL MEMOIRS — 1909–1958. Toronto: Macmillan, 1981 (David Lewis' own story of his lifetime commitment to social change and social justice).

K. McNaught, A PROPHET IN POLITICS: A BIOGRAPHY OF J. S. WOODSWORTH. Toronto: U. of T. Press, 1959 (a classic biography of a major Canadian political leader — includes information about 'the social gospel,' the 'Winnipeg General Strike,' and the birth of the CCF).

K. McNaught and D. Bercuson, THE WINNIPEG GENERAL STRIKE, 1919. Toronto: Longman Canada, 1974 (a detailed historical investigation of a key event in Canadian history).

◆ G. Montero, WE STOOD TOGETHER. Toronto: James Lorimer & Co., 1979 ('first-hand accounts of dramatic events in Canada's labour past').

D. Morton and T. Copp, WORKING PEOPLE. Ottawa: Deneau and Greenberg, 1980 (detailed history of the Canadian labour movement, photos, excellent bibliography).

K. Osborne, 'HARD-WORKING, TEMPERATE AND PEACEABLE' — THE PORTRAYAL OF WORKERS IN CANADIAN HISTORY TEXTS. Winnipeg: Monographs in Education, University of Winnipeg, 1980 (a look at what has been said — and not said! — about working people's contributions to Canadian society).

N. Penner, ed., WINNIPEG 1919: THE STRIKERS' OWN HISTORY OF THE WINNIPEG GENERAL STRIKE. Toronto: James Lorimer and Co., 1975 (how the strike was experienced by the people who accomplished it).

S. Robinson, DO NOT ERASE: THE STORY OF THE FIRST 50 YEARS OF OSSTF. Toronto: OSSTF, 1971 (historical overview of a union with which high school teachers are already familiar).

Royal Commission of the Relations of Labour and Capital

— 1889, CANADA INVESTIGATES INDUSTRIALISM. Toronto: U. of T. Press, 1973 (personal testimony of workers and employers about working conditions in the late 19th century).

S. B. Ryerson, UNEQUAL UNION. Toronto: Progress Books, 1975 (examines class and racial conflict in shaping the development of Canada — paperback).

E. Seymour, AN ILLUSTRATED HISTORY OF CANADIAN LABOUR, 1800-1974. Ottawa: CLC, 1976 (sketching our heritage, with vivid anecdotes and abundant photos).

Bob White, HARD BARGAINS: MY LIFE ON THE LINE. Toronto: McClelland and Stewart, 1988 (autobiography of Canada's most famous labour leader).

Law

J. Mather, LIVING WITH LAW: WORKING. Toronto: Community Legal Education Ontario, 1982 (curriculum for teaching high school students about workers' legal rights).

Ontario Women's Directorate, YOUR RIGHTS AS A WORKER IN ONTARIO. Toronto: Queen's Printer for Ontario, updated periodically (overview of the laws that define and protect the rights of workers).

R. D. White, LAW, CAPITALISM AND THE RIGHT TO WORK. Toronto: Garamond Press, 1986 (critical discussion of how Canadian laws deal with rights of workers, unions, etc. — paperback).

WORKING IN ONTARIO: AN EMPLOYEE'S GUIDE TO WORKPLACE LAW. Toronto: Ontario Ministry of Labour, 1990 (clear and understandable information about Ontario's workplace laws; also available in French, Italian, Portuguese, Greek and Chinese).

Literature

◆ K. Braid, COVERING ROUGH GROUND. Vancouver: Polestar, 1991 (journeywoman carpenter and poet writes about her work).

W. Freeman, SHANTYMEN OF CACHE LAKE. Toronto: James Lorimer & Co., 1975 (novel for young people, giving a view of Algonquin logging in the 1870s).

W. Freeman, LAST VOYAGE OF THE SCOTIAN. Toronto: James Lorimer & Co., 1976 (novel for young people, giving a view of the lives of Canadian sailors in the 1870s).

W. Freeman, FIRST SPRING ON THE GRAND BANKS. Toronto: James Lorimer & Co., 1978 (novel for young people, giving a view of Newfoundland fishermen in the 1870s).

E. Seymour, AN ILLUSTRATED HISTORY OF CANADIAN LABOUR, 1800–1974. Ottawa: CLC, 1976 (sketching our heritage with vivid anecdotes and abundant photos).

SHOP TALK: AN ANTHOLOGY OF POETRY. Vancouver: Pulp Press Publishers, 1985, (anthology of poetry by nine Vancouver workers).

T. Wayman, ed., GOING FOR COFFEE: POETRY ON THE JOB. Madiera Park, BC: Harbour Publishing, 1981 (anthology of excellent poems from a variety of workplaces).

◆ T. Wayman, ed., PAPERWORK: CONTEMPORARY POEMS FROM THE JOB. Madiera Park, BC: Harbour Publishing, 1991 ("a provocative sampling of the best new work writing in North America ... [by] insiders — men and women who work for a living ..."; also an important Introduction about the place of work in contemporary culture and education).

2) Magazines And Articles

CANADIAN LABOUR, quarterly publication. Ottawa: Canadian Labour Congress (free on request).

LABOUR TIMES, monthly publication. Aurora, ON: Canada Law Book Inc. (in tabloid form, covers a variety of labour-related issues and topics).

NEW INTERNATIONALIST: "Useful Work or Useless Toil — The Future of Human Labour", December 1986 issue. Toronto: New Internationalist Publications (thinking critically about work, viewing work in new ways — both in Canada and around the world; many other NI issues contain useful articles about work and workers worldwide).

OUR SCHOOLS/OUR SELVES, published six times per year. Toronto: Our Schools/Our Selves Education Foundation (focuses on educational issues of concern to working people and unions — issues of particular relevance: "It's our own knowledge: Labour, Public Education and Skills Training," Nov. '89; "What Our High Schools Could Be …," July '90 — see especially: 'History and work: Rewriting the curriculum'; "Training For What? Labour Perspectives On Job Training," Nov., '92.

OUR TIMES. published 10 times per year, Toronto: Our Times Publishing Ltd. (focuses on issues of concern to unions, the labour movement and working people).

3) Film, Video, Photography And Music

1200 MEN, video (32 minutes). NFB, 1978 (A history of the Cape Breton coal miners and their struggles in the 1920s).

P. Blood-Patterson, ed., RISE UP SINGING: THE GROUP-SINGING SONGBOOK. Bethlehem, PA: Sing Out Publications, 1988 (words and brief background notes for over 750 folk and contemporary songs, including sections on 'Hard times and blues,' 'Rich and poor,' 'Struggle' and 'Work').

◆ CANADIAN LABOUR CONGRESS AUDIO-VISUAL CATALOGUE. Ottawa: CLC, updated regularly (includes an incredibly wide array of films and videotapes relating to the labour movement, which could be included in History, English, Geography, Economics, Social Studies, Technical Studies, Business and Guidance courses).

◆ CARLTON HEIGHTS, video (29 minutes). Toronto: Ontario Federation of Labour, 1992 (a workplace health hazard provides the focus for collective action by unionized custodial workers and high school students; dramatization).

◆ CATERPILLAR: THE STORY OF A PLANT CLOSURE, video (26 minutes). Toronto: Canadian Auto Workers, 1991 — free (an account of Caterpillar workers' fight against the closure of their plant).

C. Conde and K Beveridge, FIRST CONTRACT: WOMEN AND THE FIGHT TO UNIONIZE. Toronto: Between the Lines, 1986 (photographic story of women who organized themselves).

B. Davis and B. Burron, SINGIN' ABOUT US. Toronto: James Lorimer & Co., 1976 (songs about the lives and struggles of everyday Canadians).

DEC FILMS. Toronto: Development Education Centre, updated regularly (catalogue of excellent videos and films; see especially sections on 'Labour,' 'Women — Labour,' 'Energy/Technology').

J. Dymny, THE CANADIAN WOBBLY SONGBOOK. Toronto: Canadian IWW Songbook, 1992 (a collection of new Canadian labour songs).

FINAL OFFER, 16 mm film (78 min.). NFB/CBC, 1985 (up-close look at the 1984 UAW/GM negotiations; Bob White leads Canadian members out of the UAW, to form the CAW).

E. Fowke and J. Glazer, SONGS OF WORK AND PROTEST. New York: Dover Publications, 1973 (100 songs which have been important in the North American labour movement, plus background notes for each one).

GOOD MONDAY MORNING, video (30 minutes). Toronto: Skyworks Charitable Productions & NUPGE, 1982 (about the spirit and struggles of women clerical workers across Canada).

◆ C. Heron et al, ALL THAT OUR HANDS HAVE DONE. Oakville, ON: Mosaic Press, 1981 (a photographic history of the Hamilton workers, including Sections on 'Life and Labour' and 'A Union Town').

A. Mantle, VOICES OF STRUGGLE, audio-tape. Toronto: On the Line Publishing (songs about working people and unions).

◆ MARIA, 16 mm film (47 min.), written by Rick Salutin. Toronto: CBC, 1977 (Toronto textile worker in her mid-1920s decides to try to organize a union at her workplace).

National Film Board of Canada, FILM AND VIDEO CATALOGUE. Montreal: NFB, updated yearly (check entries in the section on 'Work and Labour Relations').

◆ M. Novogrodsky et al, FRAMING OUR LIVES: PHOTOGRAPHS OF CANADIANS AT WORK. Toronto: Toronto Board of Education, 1989 (also includes a very useful teacher's guide).

E. Seymour, AN ILLUSTRATED HISTORY OF CANADIAN LABOUR, 1800–1974. Ottawa: CLC, 1976 (sketching our heritage, with vivid anecdotes and abundant photos).

SHUTDOWN, 16 mm film (27 min.). Toronto: Skyworks Charitable Foundation, 1980 (effects on women workers of Prestolite pulling out of Sarnia).

STARTING FROM NINA, 16 mm film (30 min.). Toronto: Development Education Centre, 1978 (experiences of immigrant industrial workers, working-class children, and clerical workers).

STRAIGHT FACTS, video (21 minutes). Ontario Federation of Labour and Canadian Labour Congress, mid-1980s (overview of key labour movement processes, issues, leaders and contributions to Canadian society — out of date; suggestion — use Carlton Heights instead).

♦ WHO WANTS UNIONS?, video (26 minutes). NFB, 1982 (deals with the contemporary union-busting movement in Canada, and what a non-union environment means for workers and communities).

4) *Labour Movement Resources, Contacts And Centres*

♦ CANADIAN LABOUR CONGRESS (CLC), Educational Services, 301 — 2841 Riverside Dr., Ottawa, ON, K1V 8X7, 613-521-3400.

DISTRICT LABOUR COUNCILS, in communities across Ontario (check the Yellow Pages of the phonebook, under 'Labour organizations').

LOCAL, NATIONAL and INTERNATIONAL UNIONS, in communities across Ontario (check the Yellow Pages of the phonebook, under 'Labour organizations').

METRO LABOUR EDUCATION CENTRE (MLEC). 954 King St. West, Toronto, ON M6K 1E5, 416-345-9312 (the education 'arm' of the Labour Council of Metro Toronto and York Region; variety of expertise — labour studies, labour education, labour force adjustment, ESL, literacy, human rights issues relating to work; substantial resource library).

♦ ONTARIO FEDERATION OF LABOUR (OFL), Education Department, 15 Gervais Dr., #202, Don Mills, ON, M3C 1Y8, 416-441-2731, 1-800-668-9138.

♦ WORKERS HEALTH AND SAFETY CENTRE, 15 Gervais Dr., #503, Don Mills, ON, M3C 1Y8, 416-441-1939; plus regional centres across Ontario (excellent resource for materials and speakers about workers' perspectives on health and safety in the workplace).

5) *Community-Based Contacts, Resources And Centres*

DEVELOPMENT EDUCATION CENTRE (DEC) Bookstore: 620 Bloor St. West, Toronto, ON M6G 1K7 (wide variety of recent publications and A/V materials concerning unions, the labour movement, working people, etc.)

LABOUR STUDIES PROGRAMS: Algonquin College, Carleton University, George Brown College, McMaster University, Niagara College, University of Ottawa.

LIBRARIES: Public Library, Community College and University libraries.

Ontario Women's Directorate, YOUR RIGHTS AS A WORKER IN ONTARIO. Toronto: Queen's Printer for Ontario, updated periodically.

WORKING IN ONTARIO: AN EMPLOYEE'S GUIDE TO WORKPLACE LAW. Toronto: Ontario Ministry of Labour, 1990 (clear and understandable information about Ontario's workplace laws; also available in French, Italian, Portuguese, Greek and Chinese).

UNEMPLOYMENT HELP CENTRES, in communities across Ontario (check White Pages, Yellow Pages and/or information desk at local public library).

6) *Curriculum: Lesson Plans, Teaching Strategies*

◆ W. Bigelow and N. Diamond, THE POWER IN OUR HANDS: A CURRICULUM OF THE HISTORY OF WORK AND WORKERS IN THE UNITED STATES. New York: Monthly Review Press, 1988 (a variety of powerful lessons to teach about the purposes, strategies and accomplishments of labour unions; although mainly American, many lessons are relevant to the Canadian context and classroom).

N. Gough and G. Tickner, LANGUAGE AT WORK. Holt, Rinehart and Winston of Canada, 1987 (high school text focusing on effective communication; includes readings and exercises; see especially section on 'All in a day's work'; accompanied by Teacher Resource Book).

LABOUR AND LABOUR UNIONS. Willowdale, ON: Metro Toronto School Board, 1993 — in process (extensive and detailed curriculum, aimed at Co-op courses but relevant for a variety of other courses as well).

J. Mather, LIVING WITH LAW: WORKING. Toronto: Community Legal Education Ontario, 1982 (curriculum for teaching high school students about workers' legal rights).

S. Nemiroff, WORDS ON WORK: AN INTEGRATED APPROACH TO LANGUAGE AND WORK. Toronto: Globe/Modern Curriculum Press, 1981 (lesson ideas based on working people's comments about their work; see especially unit on 'Managers and the managed')

PEOPLE AND UNIONS: THE RIGHT COMBINATION. Don Mills, ON: Ontario Federation of Labour, 1986 (a 'Speaker's Guide to Union Education', to be used with the OFL/CLC video, 'Straight Facts' — out of print and out of data — suggestion: use C. Mackay, Pay Cheques and Picket Lines, instead).

M. Siemiatycki and G. Benick, LABOUR STUDIES IN THE CLASSROOM: AN INTRODUCTION. Toronto: Labour Studies Liaison Committee of Toronto Board of Education, 1984 (pamphlet on how labour perspectives can be brought into our classrooms).

◆ R. Simon et al, LEARNING WORK: A CRITICAL PEDAGOGY OF WORK EDUCATION. New York: Bergin & Garvey, 1991 (includes chapters on 'Working knowledge,' 'Skills,' 'Occupational Health and Safety,' 'Unions,' etc.).

SOCIAL REFORM: TRADE UNIONISM. Toronto: Toronto Board of Education, Labour Studies Liaison Committee, revised 1982 (a unit of study designed for Intermediate History).

UNIONS: PART OF THEIR FUTURE. Ottawa: Canadian Labour Congress, undated (resource 'kit' for visiting speakers making presentations about unions in schools — includes lesson plans, fact sheets, pamphlets, etc.).

Jeffry Piker is an educational consultant and writer in Kingston, Ontario

Jim Turk is Education Director of the Ontario Federation of Labour, Don Mills, Ontario

**Join The Debate
On What Should Happen
In Canada's Schools.
You Can Still Get Your Own Copy
Of Each Of These Issues
Of Our Schools/Our Selves.**

Issue #1: (Journal) A Feminist Agenda For Canadian Education ... The Saskatoon Native Survival School ... School Wars: B.C., Alberta, Manitoba ... Contracting Out At The Toronto Board ... On Strike: Toronto Teachers And Saskatoon Profs ... Labour's Message In Nova Scotia Schools And Ontario ... The Free Trade Ratchet ...

Issue #2: Educating Citizens: A Democratic Socialist Agenda For Canadian Education by Ken Osborne. A coherent curriculum policy focussed on "active citizenship." Osborne takes on the issues of a "working-class curriculum" and a national "core" curriculum: what should student's know about Canada and the world at large?

Issue #3: (Journal) B.C. Teachers, Solidarity and Vander Zalm ... The Anti-Streaming Battle In Ontario ... The Dangers of School-Based Budgeting ... "Whole Language" In Nova Scotia ... Vancouver's Elementary Schools 1920-60 ... The Maritimes in Song and Text ... Teaching "G-Level" Kids ... The Squeeze On Alberta's Teachers ... In Winnipeg: "The Green Slime Strikes Back!" ...

Issue #4: (Journal) Teaching The Real Stuff Of The World: Bears, History, Work Skills ... Tory Times At Sask Ed ... The NDP At The Toronto School Board ... Indian Control In Alberta Schools ... Is The Action Affirmative For Women School Board Workers ... Radwanski: The Dark Side ... More On "Whole Language" In Nova Scotia ... A Steelworker's Education ... B.C. Teachers Hang Tough ... Decoding Discrimination ...

Issue #5: Making A People's Curriculum: The Experience Of La maîtresse d'école edited with an introduction by David Clandfield. Since 1975 this Montreal teacher collective has been producing alternative francophone curricula on labour, human rights, peace, and geo-political issues in a framework of cooperative learning. This is an anthology of their best work.

Issue #6: (Journal) Labour Education And The Auto Workers ... Nova Scotia's Children Of The State ... Patrick Watson's *Democracy* ... Popular Roots Of The "New Literacy" ... Canada's

Learner Centres ... Right-Wing Thinking In Education ... Fighting Sexism In Nfld. ... The Computer Bandwagon ... *Glasnost* and *Perestroika* Over Here? Funding Native Education ...

Issue #7: Claiming An Education: Feminism and Canadian Schools by Jane Gaskell, Arlene McLaren, Myra Novogrodsky. This book examines "equal opportunity," what students learn about women, what women learn about themselves and what has been accomplished by women who teach, as mothers and teachers.

Issue #8: It's Our Own Knowledge: Labour, Public Education & Skills Training by Julie Davis et al. The clearest expression yet of Labour's new educational agenda for the 1990s. It begins with working-class experience in the schools and community colleges, takes issue with corporate initiatives in skills training, and proposes a program "for workers, not for bosses."

Issue #9: (Journal) Rekindling Literacy In Mozambique ... Privatizing The Community Colleges ... CUPE's Educational Agenda ... High Schools & Teenage Sex ... Workers And The Rise Of Mass Schooling ... More On Nova Scotia's Children Of The State ... Grade 1 Learning ... Private School Funding ... The Globe's Attack on Media Studies ... "Consolidation" in P.E.I. ... Manitoba's High School Review ...

Issue #10: Heritage Languages: The Development And Denial Of Canada's Linguistic Resources by Jim Cummins and Marcel Danesi. This book opens up the issue of teaching heritage languages in our schools to a broad audience. It provides the historical context, analyzes opposing positions, examines the rationale and research support for heritage language promotion, and looks at the future of multiculturalism and multilingualism in Canada.

Issue #11: (Journal) No More War Toys: The Quebec Campaign ... Labelling The Under-Fives ... Building A Socialist Curriculum ... High School Streaming in Ontario ... Growing Up Male In Nova Scotia ... New Left Academics ... Tory Cutbacks In Alberta ... More On Workers And The Rise Of Mass Schooling ... The Elementary School Ruby And How High School Turned Her Sour ...

Double Issue #12-13: What Our High Schools Could Be: A Teacher's Reflections From The 60s To The 90s by Bob Davis. The author leads us where his experience has led him — as a teacher in a treatment centre for disturbed children, in an alternative community school, in a graduate education faculty, and for 23 years in two Metro Toronto high schools. The book ranges from powerful description to sharp analysis — from sex education to student streaming to the new skills mania.

Issue #14: (Journal) Feminism, Schools And The Union ... What's Happening in China's Schools ... N.B. Teacher Aides And The Struggle for Standards ... Barbie Dolls And Unicef ... Post-secondary Cuts In Alberta ... CUPE-Teacher Links ... Language Control In Nova Scotia ... Pay Equity For Ontario Teachers ... Women's Struggles/Men's Responsibility ...

Issue #15: Cooperative Learning And Social Change: Selected Writings Of Célestin Freinet edited and translated by David Clandfield and John Sivell. Célestin Freinet (1896-1966) pioneered an international movement for radical educational reform through cooperative learning. His pedagogy is as fresh and relevant today as it was in his own time, whether dealing with the importance of creative and useful work for children or linking schooling and community with wider issues of social justice and political action. This translation is the first to bring a broad selection of Freinet's work to an English-speaking audience.

Issue #16: (Journal) B.C.'s Privatization Of Apprenticeship ... Marketing Adult Ed In Saskatchewan ... The Future Of Ontario's CAATs ... Edmonton's Catalyst Theatre ... The Money Crisis In Nova Scotia Schools ... The Politics Of Children's Literature ... Tough Kids Out Of Control ... A Literacy Policy For Newfoundland? ... Métis Schooldays ... Capitalism And Donald Duck ... In Struggle: Ontario Elementary Teachers ...

Issue #17: (Journal) Towards An Anti-Racist Curriculum ... Discovering Columbus ... The Baffin Writers' Project ... The Anti-Apartheid Struggle In South Africa's Schools ... What People Think About Schooling ... Children's Work ... Radical Literacy ... Getting The Gulf Into The Classroom ... Bye-Bye Minimum C Grades ... Taking Action On AIDS ...

Issue #18: (Journal) Can The NDP Make A Difference?... Columbus In Children's Literature ... Labour Takes On Ontario's Education Bureaucrats ... Lessons From Yukon Schools ... Vision 2000 Revisited ... Getting A Feminist Education The Hard Way ... Children In Poverty ... Reflections Of A Lesbian Teacher ... Literacy, Politics and Religion In Newfoundland ... Critiquing The National Indicators ... Student Loans In Saskatchewan ...

Double Issue #19-20: Teaching For Democratic Citizenship by Ken Osborne. In this book Osborne extends his work in *Educating Citizens* and takes us through the world of modern pedagogies and the most recent research on effective teaching. He focuses particularly on "discovery learning," "critical pedagogy," and "feminist pedagogy" — drawing from a wide range of classroom practice — and builds on this foundation the key elements of an approach to teaching in which democratic citizenship is the core of student experience.

Issue #21: (Journal) The Tory Agenda ... Higher Education For Sale ... Racism and Education: Fighting Back In Nova Scotia, In A Scarborough Collegiate, In South Africa And In Victoria's Chinese Student Strike ... Saskatchewan's Neo-Conservatives ... As Neutral As My Teacher, Jesus ... "Make Work" in New Brunswick ... Teachers Politics: In Ontario And Mexico ... A Feminist Presence ... Canada's Heritage Language Programs.

Issue #22: Their Rightful Place: An Essay On Children, Families and Childcare in Canada by Loren Lind and Susan Prentice. The authors examine the complex ways we view our children in both private and public life and the care we give them inside our families and within a network of private and public childcare. They also offer an historical perspective on families and childcare in Canada and propose a strategy to develop "a free, universally accessible, publicly-funded, non-compulsory, high quality, non-profit, community-based childcare system" right across the country.

Issue #23: (Journal) Corporate Visions ... Taking On The Montreal School Commission ... Postmodern Literacy ... A Neo-Conservative Agenda In Manitoba ... Facing Up To High School Sexism ... Education In The Age Of Ecology ... An Autoworkers' Education Agenda ... Learning About Work ... The Politics Of Literacy.

Issue #24: Stacking The Deck: The Streaming Of Working Class Kids In Ontario Schools by Bruce Curtis, D.W. Livingstone & Harry Smaller. This book examines the history and structure of class bias in Ontario education. It looks at both elementary and secondary schooling and proposes a new deal for working class children. The evidence is taken from the Ontario system, but the ideas and analysis can be extended to every school in Canada.

Issue #25: (Journal) The Meaning Of Yonge Street ... What Should The NDP Do? ... New Brunswick's Plunge Into 'Excellence' ... Bargaining For Childcare ... Denmark's Efterskoles ... Reader Response And Postmodern Literacy ... Against Skills ... Slash And Burn In Nova Scotia Schools.

Issue #26: Training For What? Labour Perspectives On Job Training by Nancy Jackson et al. In this book a number of union activists analyze the corporate training agenda in Canada and open up a labour alternative. They let us see training as a tool of political struggle in the workplace, which can contribute to skill recognition, to safe and satisfying working conditions, to career progression and to building a more democratic vision of working life.

Issue #27: (Journal) NAFTA's Destruction Of Canadian Education ... The Corporate Hijacking Of Canada's Universities .... Lining Up Gender In Elementary School ... Totems and Taboos In Bilingual Education ... Teaching Outside The Mainstream ... The Nuclear Agenda In Saskatchewan's Schools ... The Anti-Racist Uses Of To Kill A Mockingbird ... New Brunswick Reading Circles ... John Dewey And American Democracy ... Surveying Canada's Teens ... Educating For Change.

Issue #28: Schools And Social Justice by R.W. Connell. Throughout this broad analysis, which spans the educational systems of Europe, North America and Australia, Connell argues that the issue of social justice is fundamental to what good education is about. If the school system deals unjustly with some of its pupils, the quality of education for all of the others is degraded. He calls for "curricular justice," which opens out the perspective of the least advantaged, roots itself in a democratic context, and moves toward the creation of a more equalitarian society.

Issue #29: (Journal) Teaching Mi'kmaq: Living A Language ... TV And The Dene ... Turning A Blind Eye To Linguistic Genocide ... After 1492–1992: A Post-Colonial Supplement For The Canadian Curriculum ... The Emerging Corporate Agenda For Canadian High Schools ... A Critical Look At The Skills Mania ... Show Boat: Reflections On The Passage Of A Racist Icon ... The Ninth OISE Survey: The Public Mood In Tough Times ... A New Vision For Bilingual Education.

Issue #30: Pandora's Box: Corporate Power, Free Trade and Canadian Education by John Calvert and Larry Kuehn. The authors lay bare the real story behind corporate interest in education and show, via a detailed analysis of the NAFTA text and political and economic trends throughout North America, how NAFTA is being used by Corporate Canada in their attempts to commercialize and privatize public education.

Issue #31: (Journal) The NDP and Education: What Happened In Ontario, B.C., Saskatchewan, and Manitoba? ... N.B.'s Strategy For Post-Secondary Education ... Gender Equity: A Personal Journey ... American Racism, Canadian Surrender: More Reflections On "To Kill A Mockingbird" ... A Letter From Siberia ... All The News That's Fit For Business: YNN Zeroes In On The Canadian Classroom ... Speak It! From The Heart Of Black Nova Scotia ... Educating The English.

Subscribe Now!

Here's What's Coming In Future Issues Of Our Schools/Our Selves

Articles On:

What Do We Tell Our Kids About Canada — Science And Standardized Testing — Environmental Activism — Unionizing ESL Teachers — A Winnipeg Inner City School — The World Of Teenage Girls — The B.C. School Wars Continue — Labour, Education And The Arts — Sex In Upper Canada's Classrooms — Young Women In Trades — Education Politics In Alberta — Inside The Labelling Process — Schools And Museums — Whatever Happened To York University?

You'll get three journals and three books a year for each subscription.

Books On:

Sex in School — Teaching History — Don't Tell Us It Can't Be Done: Alternative Classrooms At Work — A Socialist-Feminist Approach To Phys. Ed. — Native Control Of White Education — Whatever Happened To High School History? — From Multiculturalism To Anti-Racism Studies — Australian Education Activism — What's Basic? A Citizen's Guide To The Battle For Ontario Education — Racism and Education — Where Is The U.S. Left In Education? — What Do People Really Think About Our Schools? — An Anti-Racist Curriculum For Nova Scotia

It's a great bargain, as much as 50% off the newstand price.

OUR SCHOOLS / OUR SELVES

Bringing together education activists in our schools, our communities and our unions...*with your help* !

Please enter my subscription for 6 issues of OUR SCHOOLS/OUR SELVES starting with issue number_____. Please check one:

INDIVIDUAL		ORGANIZATION	
____ Regular rate	$34.00	____ In Canada	$50.00
____ Student/Unemployed/		____ Outside Canada	Cdn $60.00
Pensioner rate	$28.00	**SUSTAINING**	
____ Outside Canada	Cdn $46.00	____ $100 ____ $200 Other $____	

OR send me issue number(s) _____ at $9.00 per single and $16.00 per double issue

Name_____

Address_____

City_____ Prov_____ Code_____

Occupation_____

___ Cheque enclosed   ___ Bill me later   ___ VISA / Mastercard

Card No_____Expiry date _____

Signature_____

Subscribe Today

OUR SCHOOLS / OUR SELVES

Bringing together education activists in our schools, our communities and our unions...*with your help* !

Please enter my subscription for 6 issues of OUR SCHOOLS/OUR SELVES starting with issue number_____. Please check one:

INDIVIDUAL		ORGANIZATION	
____ Regular rate	$34.00	____ In Canada	$50.00
____ Student/Unemployed/		____ Outside Canada	Cdn $60.00
Pensioner rate	$28.00	**SUSTAINING**	
____ Outside Canada	Cdn $46.00	____ $100 ____ $200 Other $____	

OR send me issue number(s) _____ at $9.00 per single and $16.00 per double issue

Name_____

Address_____

City_____ Prov_____ Code_____

Occupation_____

___ Cheque enclosed   ___ Bill me later   ___ VISA / Mastercard

Card No_____Expiry date _____

Signature_____

Pass to a friend

**Business
Reply Mail**

No postage stamp
necessary if mailed
in Canada.

Postage will be paid by

49261

OUR SCHOOLS/OUR SELVES
1698 Gerrard Street East,
Toronto, Ontario, CANADA
M4L 9Z9

**Business
Reply Mail**

No postage stamp
necessary if mailed
in Canada.

Postage will be paid by

49261

OUR SCHOOLS/OUR SELVES
1698 Gerrard Street East,
Toronto, Ontario, CANADA
M4L 9Z9